Children's Homes Revisited

of related interest

Young People Leaving Care
Life After the Children Act
Edited by Bob Broad
ISBN 1 85302 412 0

**Child Welfare Services Developments in Law,
Policy, Practice and Research**
Edited by Malcom Hill and Jane Aldgate
ISBN 1 85302 316 7

Good Practice in Child Protection
A Manual for Professionals
Edited by Hilary Owen and Jacki Pritchard
ISBN 1 85302 205 5

Child Psychiatric Units
At the Crossroads
Edited by Rosemary Chesson and Douglas Chisholm
ISBN 1 85302 329 9

Children's Homes Revisited

David Berridge and Isabelle Brodie

Jessica Kingsley Publishers
London and Philadelphia

First published in the United Kingdom in 1998 by
Jessica Kingsley Publishers Ltd
116 Pentonville Road
London N1 9JB, England
and
1900 Frost Road, Suite 101
Bristol, PA 19007, U S A

Library of Congress Cataloging in Publication Data
A CIP catalogue record for this book is available from the Library of Congress

British Library Cataloguing in Publication Data
A CIP catalogue record for this book is available from the British Library

ISBN 1 85302 565 8

Printed and Bound in Great Britain by
Athenaeum Press, Gateshead, Tyne and Wear

Contents

Acknowledgements

Numerous people have contributed to the completion of this research and it is possible here to thank only some of them. Most of all we are indebted to children and staff in the sample of homes for allowing us glimpses of their lives and situations. It is hoped that we were unobtrusive yet have been able to convey accurately what we observed and were told. Managers were also very co-operative in allowing us access to homes in what tends to be a controversial area of service. We cannot name them for reasons of anonymity. We are grateful to the University of Luton for supporting this work financially and in many other ways. Kate Robinson, especially, has been highly positive in her approach to research. David Barrett, our head of department, has also been very helpful. Several people read the manuscript at draft stage and fed back useful comments: Lesley Archer, Michael Little, Carol Robinson, John Rowlands and Ian Sinclair. We have also benefited from collaboration with NSPCC researchers Pat Cawson and Christine Barter, together with colleagues in Luton and Bedfordshire social services as well as a number of other agencies. Luton psychology colleagues Tony Canavan and Jessica Bennett offered welcome methodological and statistical advice. Any shortcomings in what follows of course remain our responsibility. Finally, we would like to thank Pauline Rajaram for secretarial and administrative help. Librarians at the University of Luton, particularly Dawn McGerty, and at the National Children's Bureau also played a valuable part.

David Berridge
Isabelle Brodie

I

Background and Introduction

Sequels are a rare commodity in the academic literature. There are a small number of cohort studies, such as the National Child Development Study which focused on all those born within a particular week in the late 1950s and has researched their progress at regular intervals since (Ferri and Smith 1996; Fogelman 1976). In the child welfare literature there are also some – not enough – valuable longitudinal studies of children separated from their parents which report on them at different times (Millham *et al.* 1986; Quinton and Rutter 1984). However, studies are scarce which set out to address systematically the development of a service or an institution over a period.

This book is an exception. It analyses changes in the structure and use of residential child care services over a decade. This is done by revisiting the scene depicted in 1985 in the study *Children's Homes* (Berridge 1985). The original investigation examined residential services provided for children and young people living in three local authorities in different regions of England. In particular, it comprised a detailed study of the occupants, workforce and regime of 20 children's homes of contrasting types. As we shall see, many developments have occurred in children's homes in the intervening decade but the perceived nature and implications of these changes have been based too often on conjecture rather than on detailed empirical study. The situation of some of society's most damaged and vulnerable citizens warrants more careful scrutiny.

This study, therefore, revisits the same three local authorities some ten years later and contrasts systematically residential child care services offered on each occasion. Homes that have closed are substituted with others that reflect current patterns of use. Compared with the earlier period, we set out to discover what changes have taken place in this sector and for what reasons. Who now lives in children's homes and why? Who works there? How is this national sample of homes organised and run? What are staff and young people's views on residential child care? What contacts do young people and homes maintain with families and with other professionals, such as colleagues in education? In addition, compared with the original study, which was more descriptive, it is now possible to analyse in greater detail the quality of care offered within homes and to identify from our data which variables seem to facilitate or hinder this.

As shown in the original volume, the residential care of children is a subject that has long been tinged with controversy and public concern. Historically, as now, we should not assume that altruism has been the only motive in providing welfare services, and there has been a strong moral and political dimension throughout care provision (Frost and Stein 1989). For example, with the growth of industrialisation in the nineteenth century, attention focused on the control of what were perceived as the 'dangerous classes' and future generations of the urban poor. Both physical and social stigmas were linked with institutional care under the Poor Law and interventions were not genuinely life-enhancing, nor were they intended to be (Pinchbeck and Hewitt 1973). Few would publicly espouse such sentiments today yet, significantly, unsympathetic views are to be heard more frequently in the 1990s than in the build up to the previous study a decade earlier.

Although attitudes today may generally be more benign than throughout much of history, it is likely that this legacy continues to exert some influence on the structure and delivery of residential services. Despite various efforts, residential care has continued to be seen as the poor relation of social work. It has lower status and its workforce is less well professionally equipped. Young people who are resident are very much aware of the negative public stereotypes of the children's homes' population (NCC/*Who Cares?* Trust 1993). Reports of unruliness and delinquency associated with homes feature frequently in the local media to the considerable annoyance of neighbours and councillors alike. Nationally, revelations of past abuse of residents by staff surface with alarming regularity. Some are sceptical about whether children's homes continue to have relevant functions as residents become older, length of stay shorter and the value base more dissipated (Gooch 1996). The service is perceived to be inordinately expensive. The outlook for unskilled youths in an increasingly competitive labour market seems bleak. As a consequence, some social services departments have decided to abandon residential care and, where necessary, buy in places from neighbouring authorities or the private sector.

This dissatisfaction is the backcloth against which our study commenced. In this opening chapter we review some of the important developments to have occurred over the past decade that are likely to have influenced the situation of children's homes. Initially, we refer to the series of crises that have been reported. We then discuss changing patterns of service use, which is followed by developments in policy and the law. Next, we turn to more general social factors affecting children and parents. We then summarise findings from key research studies.

Crises in residential child care

The long-standing structural weaknesses identified earlier are likely to have played at least some part in a series of crises and scandals afflicting a range of residential establishments over the last decade, some of which highlight serious malpractice perhaps 10 or even 20 years earlier (Berridge and Brodie 1996). These rocked public and professional confidence in residential child care and have served to undermine what progress might otherwise have been made. Recent episodes to emerge include insidious activities of groups of paedophiles who gained access to abuse children sexually while employed in residential homes in north Wales and the north-west of England (*The Times* 1996). Similar reports arose earlier concerning the abuse of residents in the Kincora boys' hostel in East Belfast (Department of Health and Social Services Northern Ireland 1986). The late Frank Beck had also been convicted on 17 counts of sexual and physical assaults against children while officer in charge of various children's homes in Leicestershire between 1973 and 1986 (Kirkwood 1993). In addition, there were the disconcerting conditions found by school inspectors at the Crookham Court boarding school in Berkshire.

All of these cases, and a number of others, attracted considerable media attention and did little to boost the morale and self-confidence of an already beleaguered service. But the experiences that perhaps captured public imagination the most were those stemming from what has become known as 'Pindown': a form of regime which operated in homes in Staffordshire between 1983 and 1989 (Levy and Kahan 1991). Under a distorted form of 'behaviour modification', children had been confined to barely furnished rooms for long periods and forced to wear night clothes during the day; deprived of contact and stimulus; and prohibited from going out. One hundred and thirty-two children aged between 9 and 17 years had been subjected to this treatment.

One of the most disconcerting, perhaps even unfathomable, aspects of 'Pindown' was that it had all been conducted quite openly. The inquiry report (Levy and Kahan 1991) painstakingly detailed the context within the county that had enabled the regime to flourish, and it sometimes seems, as with similar crises, that it would be difficult to create an environment in which serious malpractice were more likely to occur if one had set out deliberately to do so. A number of common themes have been identified from some of these inquiry reports, relating to management, policy and practice issues (Berridge and Brodie 1996). These include inadequate line management; minimal direct management contact with children and staff; unsatisfactory placement policies and processes; inadequate recruitment processes and staff training; reluctance to use secure provision and more specialised alternative services; inadequate or no external expert advice; and, lest we should overlook the rather obvious fact that most of these scandals are committed directly by men, the presence of 'macho' or masculine charisma or culture. Others should beware if this configuration of problems exists elsewhere.

Changing patterns of service use

These developments occurred during, and no doubt contributed to, a period of significantly changing use of the residential child care sector. As in all walks of life, we should be cautious about the use of statistics, and researchers have warned that static snapshots of services, rather than looking at use over time and throughputs, can give a distorted view (Millham *et al.* 1986; Rowe, Hundleby and Garnett 1989). Nonetheless, comparing like with like, Figure 1.1 reveals a considerable change in the pattern of use of child care services between 1985 and 1995.

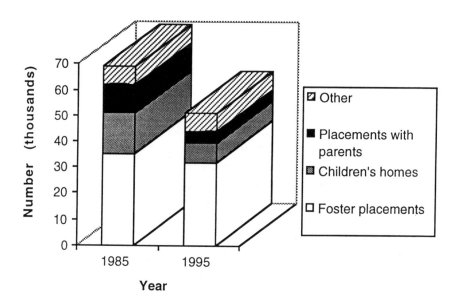

Figure 1.1 Children looked after by local authorities, 1985–95, England

The total number of children looked after by English local authorities fell over the decade by approximately 30 per cent, from nearly 70,000 in 1985 to 49,000 in 1995. Within this the number fostered dropped by some 2000. However, the figure living in children's homes on any one day more than halved from over 16,000 to 7700. These overall changes also mask interesting developments between groups of residential homes. For example, local authority-managed facilities declined substantially in line with overall changes. The voluntary sector also shrank from over 4000 in the early 1980s to barely 600 in 1995, a major change in its traditional institutional role (Parker 1990). Official statistics record the number of children placed in privately registered homes staying about constant over the decade at approximately 650 placements at any one time (Department of Health 1996a). However, this appears to be an underestimate. Figures for 1995 put the number of private homes at approximately 180, a sixth of the total (Department of Health 1996b).

A survey of residential child care in the 12 European Union countries and Sweden revealed that the declining use in the UK is part of a broader trend as a variety of alternative services develop (Madge 1994). Disconcertingly, however, it argued that seldom among our neighbours is there the same sense of pessimism and crisis. Obviously, services have different historical traditions. The general reduction in institutional care has been reported also in the United States although some, fortunately isolated, voices have advocated a 'bring back the orphanage' campaign to be funded by more punitive approaches towards the recipients of welfare (Smith 1995).

Statistics published for England offer some further interesting insights. For example, the average number of residents per home has fallen from over ten in 1985 to under seven a decade later (Berridge 1985; Department of Health 1996b). In addition, the total number of 1139 residential homes in 1985 includes 86 registered residential care homes, mostly catering for children with learning, physical and sensory impairments. Significantly, and related to the previous point, the presentation of official statistics shows separately children accommodated in an agreed series of short-term placements ('respite care') under Section 20 of the Children Act 1989. In the past this has tended to apply to disabled children, although new patterns of planned accommodation may be emerging as wider forms of family support (Aldgate, Bradley and Hawley 1996). However, a key point for the discussion at this stage is that very significant numbers of disabled children are accommodated in residential establishments under these planned arrangements and this category of placements is often overlooked in general debates. Indeed, at any one time there are some 1200 children and young people accommodated in this way (about the same number are also in foster homes), which therefore comprises a sixth of the total residential population (Department of Health 1996b). This will develop into an important theme for this research.

Before leaving the statistics, we should also add that the above analysis does not specifically mention small unregistered children's homes providing for three or fewer children. A study by the Social Services Inspectorate (Department of Health 1995b) identified 118 homes offering places to some 250 children. Standards of care were felt to be variable and important concerns were raised, including the placement of some very young children considerable distances from their families. It is felt that the small unregistered homes raise quite specific issues which merit separate study and so our research did not include them.

Developments in policy and the law

To give credit where it is due, a wide range of strategies was employed by government to try to raise standards in the residential sector and prevent scandals from reoccurring. It is, of course, a pity that a very serious situation had to be reached before such positive measures were deployed. As we shall see, steps taken concerned the law, policy and practice, staffing and research. Evidence discussed later will provide some testimony as to whether these efforts have led to raised standards.

Soon after the publication of the 'Pindown' report in 1991, the Secretary of State for Health announced a detailed review of residential child care in England. The subsequent publication, which became known, after its author, as the 'Utting Report', set out a comprehensive overview of child care services and a series of well-received conclusions and recommendations (Department of Health 1991a). The report emphasised that residential care is an essential service and set out the circumstances in which it was felt that it is most appropriately used: namely, primarily for adolescents who, euphemistically, 'may present challenging behaviour'; for those where foster care has failed or is otherwise inappropriate; with siblings who otherwise could not be kept together; and for those who have been seriously damaged and require special help. Recommendations covered issues related to the welfare of children, management and resources, including the pay and conditions of residential staff.

A similar review was undertaken in Wales (Social Services Inspectorate, Wales and Social Information Systems 1991). Its general analysis was along the same lines as 'Utting' but its tone was even more forthright. The report bluntly described residential care as, 'a marginal unspecific activity taking those whose needs the rest of the system fails to meet' (p. 11). Thus most admissions were said to be unplanned and to occur in crisis. It was revealed that the only consistent policy statement about the use of children's homes in Wales was that it should be a short-term option: 'the implication must be that the children's home experience is a damaging one and must be kept to a minimum' (p. 11). Staff were felt to be lacking essential skills and training and the objectives set were often mutually incompatible. The most critical remarks were reserved for attempts to deal with challenging behaviour:

> The review revealed a substantial failure to meet the needs of this group. The attention of the staff was diverted to deal with other conflicting demands. Homes which provide a service of this kind need to be staffed by highly skilled people who are well trained at the outset and supported by continuing training and extensive and intensive backup from other professionals and within their own professional support system. There is no more professionally demanding task in the social services field than this and it can only be handled at the highest level of skill (p.12).

As the fieldwork for our research commenced, it seemed that our findings would mirror closely those of the Welsh report. However, this may have been due to our starting point, which was a group of local authority homes dealing with adolescents. As our fieldwork widened, geographically as well as to take in other categories of provision, our experiences were fortunately more varied.

Also in 1991, following the conviction of Frank Beck in Leicester, a committee of inquiry was set up, chaired by Norman Warner, to examine the selection and recruitment methods and criteria for staff working in children's homes (Department of Health 1992). Again, this was a very comprehensive exercise resulting in over 80 recommendations. These spanned recruitment procedures, application forms, advertising, employee references, interviewing, police checks, performance appraisal, training and support.

The extent of activity on child care issues is reflected also in the fact that, at the same time as the above, a substantial new piece of legislation was being implemented, the Children Act 1989. This constituted a major overhaul of private and public law for children and families, which was generally well received (Packman and Jordan 1991). The Act strongly endorsed the view that children are best looked after within their families. Parental responsibility would be retained even when family breakdown occurred, and 'partnership with parents' became a key theme. Local authorities have a duty to assist families with 'children in need' and this responsibility includes other agencies such as education, health and housing, and not just social services. Disabled children were included as one category of children in need and, therefore, were incorporated in mainstream legislation for all children. Administrative measures to restrict parents' access to children and powers of recovery were abolished and, instead, a legal route was required. The process of obtaining emergency orders was made more stringent for professionals. Children themselves must be consulted directly about matters affecting them and are to be separately legally represented in court. Local authorities must also pay regard to children's religion, racial origin, and cultural and linguistic background. Complaints procedures have to be developed and publicised.

The legislation included a range of other measures to which it would be impossible to do justice here (Department of Health 1989). However, apart from the specific details, it is also relevant to locate the Children Act 1989 in the context of other social policy initiatives at the time. This was a period of Conservative governments in which there were restraints in public expenditure, business principles were introduced into public services and there was a general distrust of independent experts. Some observers, such as Parton (1991), have portrayed the 1989 legislation as quite consistent with other social reforms of the 1980s and 1990s. He argued that the professional knowledge base and autonomy of social work were diluted by making it more mechanistic and legalistic. In addition, one could highlight the emphasis on *responsibilities* rather than *rights*. In relation to child protection specifically, there was also more focus on the need to avoid unwarranted intrusion in the family (Home Office *et al.* 1991), which would be warmly applauded by those on the Right mistrustful of social workers, especially following the events in Cleveland (Butler-Sloss 1988).

In contrast, our view is that the Children Act 1989 was probably unlike any other social policy legislation of the 1980s (Berridge 1995b; Packman and Jordan 1991). It made no mention of business principles or market forces. There were no explicit references to privatisation or 'purchaser–provider' splits. The rhetoric of consumer 'choice' was also absent. It was highly child-centred and, in Fox Harding's (1991) useful conceptualisation of approaches in child welfare, reflected both the *defence of birth families and parents' rights* and *children's rights* perspectives. Most significantly, perhaps, the Act did not signify a diminution in the role and responsibilities of the state. Furthermore, compared with much recent social policy, its key messages were based on, and consistent with, research messages (discussed later in this chapter). Political challenges to the Act and the values it embodied did not begin to materialise until, predictably perhaps, the run-up to the 1997 general election.

The 1989 legislation was accompanied by nine detailed volumes of guidance, which set out in greater detail its implications in specific areas. Volume 4 dealt exclusively with residential care and contained much sensible practice guidance on topics including staffing and staff support; the physical environment of children's homes; aspects of daily care; planning and review processes; family contact; aftercare; and secure provision (Department of Health 1991b). Another, Volume 6, brought together current thinking about services for disabled children and their families (Department of Health 1991c). Following the unacceptable containment of children in homes in Staffordshire under the 'Pindown' regime, the Department of Health (1993) also bravely tackled the controversial subject of permissible forms of control in residential care. This written guidance has been criticised for being too general but contained sensible principles and suggestions for good practice that should assist agencies and individual establishments in maintaining order. It specified that children could only be physically restrained to prevent significant injury to any person or serious damage to property. As we shall see, this became a key issue in several of the homes we visited and we return to this topic in Chapter 5 (see also Department of Health 1997).

Wider social factors

Children's homes of course do not exist in a vacuum and their functioning will be influenced by a variety of wider social factors. The nature of this relationship, however, is complex and insufficiently understood. For example, reviewing long-term historical trends, Parker and Loughran (1990) concluded that the number of children in public care seems to be more closely linked to supply-led factors and what can be afforded, rather than levels of need (see also Gooch 1996). Thus at times of high unemployment there are often fewer, not more, children looked after away from home as one might expect.

Encouragingly, during the past decade there has been greater discussion and awareness of children's rights and we might, therefore, expect this to have been translated into improvements in their welfare. Like all other countries in the European Union, the UK signed the United Nations Convention on the Rights of the Child (United Nations 1989). This stipulates that, because of their vulnerability, children require special care and protection. This applies particularly to those deprived of their family environment (Article 20). However, a subsequent audit of children's rights in the UK by a UN Committee aroused government displeasure somewhat by being strongly critical across many areas of social policy (*The Times* 1995). The Children Act 1989 was positively welcomed but, for example, the extent of child poverty, homelessness among the young and plans to set up secure training centres for 12–14-year-old persistent offenders were strongly criticised.

Other sources paint a disconcerting picture of children's experiences in the 1980s and 1990s (Berridge 1995a). Though the exact effects on children are complicated, few welcome the fact that some three in every five marriages now seem destined for breakdown (Haskey 1996). Even for those that remain intact, the quality of parenting which children receive is highly variable. Halsey (1992) has described this period as one of 'low fertility and low morality', and he argues that men in particular, by embracing individualised values, are increasingly putting their own needs before those of the young. A recent survey showed how little time many modern fathers spend with their children: sports and hobbies played larger parts in men's lives than bringing up the young (Parsons 1995). We should be cautious of retrospective accounts, but a Barnardo's (1995) survey revealed that three in five adults thought generally the world today is a worse place than when they were young.

Bradshaw's (1990) authoritative review of child poverty and deprivation in the UK concluded that:

> During the 1980s children have borne the brunt of the changes that have oc-curred in the economic conditions, demographic structure and social policies of the UK. More children have been living in low income families and the number of children living in poverty has doubled. Inequalities have also become wider. (p.5; see also Bradshaw 1996; Kumar 1993).

In this period, resources were transferred away from families with children to those without, and proportionately more children were shown to live in poverty than did adults. Almost one in three children now live in households with no one in a full-time job (Government Statistical Service 1996).

Especially pertinent for adolescents, research has demonstrated that, due to a range of social and economic factors, young people's transition to adulthood has become significantly more difficult and complicated than in the past (Morrow and Richards 1996). This includes changing trends in education, training and employment, as well as restrictions on the availability of social security benefits. Consequently, young people are frequently economically dependent on their families until well into their mid-20s and there is an increased tendency for expectations and ambitions to be frustrated. Interestingly, this seems to apply particularly to males: 41 per cent of childless men between the ages of 20 and 34 have been reported as still living at home with their parents, compared with 25 per cent for women (Mintel 1996). It may be thought that prolonging adolescence in this way would lead to increased offending among young men, yet continuing to live at home, specifically, seems to have the opposite effect (Graham and Bowling 1995).

It is well documented that children looked after by local authorities originate from the poorest sections of society and their families have witnessed multiple social and economic disadvantages (Bebbington and Miles 1989; Department of Health 1991d). The deterioration in social conditions outlined above is likely to have led to increased levels of stress in families. Though the intermediate mechanisms are complex, one would expect this to influence the overall numbers of children in need and the severity of problems that individuals face. Correspondingly it seems that, compared with their predecessors, children's homes' residents in the 1990s are unlikely to have fewer problems or be easier to work with – quite the opposite.

Child care research

Having surveyed the wider scene, we now turn our attention to social work once more. The remainder of this chapter discusses research on children in need undertaken over the past decade that is likely to be relevant to the current study. There is particular focus on residential child care.

Children's Homes (1985)

It is necessary at this stage to give further details about the original 1985 *Children's Homes* study. As stated earlier, this comprised a detailed examination of 20 children's homes in three local authorities in different regions of England. The main research method used was a period of participant observation spent in each home, supplemented by other forms of data collection. It was discovered that slightly more boys than girls were living in the homes and, significantly, two-fifths of residents were living with one or more siblings. The average age of young people was 14 years. A variety of factors propelled young people into public care, the most common of which were neglect or injury of the child and their behavioural problems at home. Four broad categories of residents were identified. First, there was a group of younger siblings recently admitted to accommodation and for whom this was a first and temporary placement. This comprised approximately one in ten of the total population. A second category – about half the overall group – were those awaiting long-stay placements, usually with foster families. Indeed, a third of all residents in the 20 homes had already experienced one or more breakdowns in planned long-term foster placements. The third group, in some ways the most hapless, had been separated from parents most, if not all, of their lives and had witnessed an assortment of unsuccessful substitute family placements. A fifth of residents came into this group and the care system had failed them. The final quarter of residents constituted adolescents, mostly girls, who had recently left home but maintained regular, if somewhat volatile, links with parents.

Many staff working in the 20 homes in the original study had considerable experience of child care work, though few had experienced relevant professional training. They often complained of being professionally and socially isolated (nearly all heads of homes lived in their establishments, as did about a third of their colleagues). Staff were hard working, generally well motivated and the calibre of recent recruits especially seemed impressive. Three types of children's homes were depicted according to size and leadership style: small, traditional 'family group'-style homes; medium size 'adolescent hostels'; and the larger 'multi-purpose' homes.

Five main functions of children's homes for the wider child care system were identified: reception into public care; as a safety net for fostering failures; for young people maintaining strong family loyalties; as a resource for those who reject fostering; and in keeping together or reuniting sibling groups. Although it was felt by the researchers and young people alike that the quality of individual care offered in homes was generally satisfactory, a main conclusion of the original research was that there was not a rational allocation of children with particular problems to the homes best suited to meet them. These and other findings will be returned to throughout this study in order to examine changes in residential child care over the past decade.

Other studies

We are fortunate in that the 1980s and 1990s have been periods in which child care researchers have been very active: this brief overview, therefore, must be unavoidably selective. Unlike most social policy legislation of the decade, the Children Act 1989 was solidly based on findings from a coherent and planned programme of research. This demonstrated, for example, that there were often barriers to contact between parents and absent children, planning was inadequate and there was too great a reliance on compulsory and emergency measures (Department of Health and Social Security 1985). Further research summaries have followed (Department of Health 1991d), including the useful volume pulling together the messages from a body of child protection research. This stressed that there has been too much social work emphasis on investigation of abuse and too little on family support and dealing with its aftermath (Department of Health 1995a). Parton (1996) has criticised this body of work as demonstrating insufficient insight into the tensions and realities of child protection work in the current social and political context. Government also supported a valuable programme of work, the *Looking After Children* initiative, clarifying the nature of outcomes in child care and how to measure them (Parker *et al.* 1991). This has been translated into tools for practitioners to plan for children and monitor their progress (Ward 1995).

Research, long overdue, also focused specifically on the needs of adolescents (Department of Health 1996c). A National Children's Bureau study examined the complex area of assessment, including the respective roles for foster and residential care (Sinclair, Garnett and Berridge 1995). Triseliotis and colleagues (1995) highlighted the absence of strategies and family support services concerning adolescents. Little use was made of foster care by their sample and the overall impression of children's homes was generally positive, although interestingly less so than with residential special schools for children with emotional and behavioural difficulties (see also Grimshaw with Berridge 1994). Research continued to document the highly precarious situation of care leavers and the variability in aftercare services on offer (Biehal *et al.* 1992)3.

Relevant to this study, Parker, Loughran and Gordon (1992) investigated the subject of disabled children living in residential care. As we shall see, this raises important conceptual and policy issues since the work, based on further analysis of the Office of Population, Censuses and Surveys' data, included behaviour problems as a form of impairment. Defined in this way, well over a third – 37 per cent – of all school-age children 'in care' in England in the late 1980s and living in residential units were 'disabled'.

Additional attention was focused in the 1980s and 1990s on services for disabled children and their families. The Department of Health Social Services Inspectorate's (1994a) review of services in four authorities revealed a mixed picture. Partnership with parents was said to work well in two authorities but less so in the others. Insufficient information was provided for families and consultation with children specifically was inadequate. Each authority needed to do more to develop culturally sensitive services. Parents whose children received short-term care spoke positively of its benefits.

Research into the implementation of the Children Act 1989 for disabled children included six short-term care homes (Robinson, Weston and Minkes

1994). This demonstrated that the situation had moved on from the very bleak portrayal in the 1980s by Oswin (1984). The evaluators were reported to be impressed by the overall level of commitment and care provided by staff in the six homes. Information provided to users and their families had improved. Planning for transition to adult services had also progressed. In agreement with the Social Services Inspectorate findings, however, homes had made inadequate attempts to consult children about their feelings in relation to short-term care. Staff training was very variable, including the issue of cultural awareness. Procedures needed to be improved for child care plans and reviews. Importantly, the vast majority of children were found to enjoy using these short-term services, although a minority were unhappy about the arrangements (see also Robinson 1996a, b).

As in previous decades, and paradoxically given its significance, foster care attracted little specific attention from researchers (Berridge 1997). The residential sector, however, continued to support a veritable industry. Researchers – transitory, marginal, socially remote and with limited career prospects – must feel a certain affinity with the adolescent in group care. A useful summary of residential care research was written in the early 1990s (Bullock, Little and Millham 1993a). This developed thinking on theoretical approaches to residential care. It also identified the need for more 'quality assessments' of residential life. Gaps in knowledge included the effects of the Children Act 1989 and the impact of residence on particular sub-groups of children.

Further research on the important issue of the *costs* of residential care was undertaken by Knapp and Robinson (1989). This revealed, for example, that calculations of the comparative costs of foster and residential care are often simplistic and do not compare like with like. When children's homes are contrasted with specialist or professional foster care, which is often the realistic alternative, the difference in costs persists but is much narrower than is generally perceived.

Another strand of research over the past decade, relevant to our current work, concerns the *use* of residential child care facilities. We saw earlier the general numerical decline in children's home placements, which has international parallels. Despite this, studies have continued to show that children's homes are used regularly as young people pass through the care system. Thus Rowe *et al.*'s (1989) major survey of child care placements found that, over the two-year study period, broadly similar numbers of foster and residential placements occurred. For adolescents specifically, the latter were three times as prevalent. Surprisingly perhaps, a quarter of all placements for the under 11s were in residential care. Two Scottish studies have similarly revealed that, for teenagers living away from home, residential placements were the most common option (Kendrick 1995; Triseliotis *et al.* 1995).

The *effectiveness* of residential care has been a subject that has attracted increasing attention over the decade. Interestingly, compared with the rather negative appraisal of children's homes outlined earlier in this chapter, research findings do not indicate that alternative interventions are demonstrably superior (Berridge 1994). To date, however, our ability to measure child-related outcomes has been limited, although this is now changing following the thinking underpinning the *Looking After Children* initiative. Previously, therefore, much evaluation of outcomes tended to be service-related rather than child-specific. An exception is Colton (1988), who compared the progress of matched samples of young people in children's homes and specialist foster care. On various dimensions he concluded that similar improvement was made for both groups. Rowe *et al.* (1989), using a variety of measures by which social workers were asked to rate placements, also concluded that for comparable groups of children the perceived 'success' was broadly similar. Kendrick's (1995) work in Scotland reached the same conclusion.

Warwickshire was the first local authority nationally to cease to have any residential child care of its own and a detailed evaluation of its services focused on a sample of young people who, elsewhere, would have been likely candidates for children's homes (Cliffe with Berridge 1991). The report emphasised the significance of a historical understanding of Warwickshire's policy decisions – it didn't have very much residential care in the first place. Other findings included the fact that the authority had not saved any money by pursuing its non-residential approach, nor had it set out to do so. Importantly, the county continued to use some residential care but provided by other agencies. 'Outcomes' for children in Warwickshire were broadly comparable with findings from other research studies undertaken in areas where residential care remained an option. However, there was a lack of choice of foster carers and, at the time, few children from minority ethnic groups were able to be placed with families of the same cultural background. An official national inspection discovered that these problems still affected foster care in the mid-1990s (Department of Health Social Services Inspectorate 1996).

In addition to a Social Services Inspectorate (1994a) report on residential child care provided in the early 1990s in 11 local authorities, there are a number of other reports relating to specific areas, such as children's educational experiences. We refer to these in the following chapters as relevant points are being discussed.

However, the final study to be introduced here is probably the most important and this is Sinclair and Gibbs' (1996) work. This extensive research analysed the care provided to over 220 children living in 48 children's homes in England. It covers the purpose of placements, factors associated with high quality provision and, by following up residents over a six-month period, examines the relationship between the residential experience and subsequent development. The perspectives of children, parents, social workers, heads of homes and other residential staff are included. The main factors associated with good quality care in Sinclair and Gibbs' research were three-fold: homes that were small; where heads of homes were 'empowered' – that is, where roles were clear and heads of homes were given the autonomy to get on with the job; and where there was staff agreement. Interestingly, better staff ratios or homes with more qualified staff were not linked to improved care. Another important finding was that the experiences of good quality care seemed to be transitory and did not lead to better outcomes for children six months later. Clearly there is overlap between this research and our own, and regular comparisons will be made in the following text, including consequences for policy and practice.

Having outlined other researchers' recent work, the remainder of this report will now concentrate on our own. Chapter 2 explains how our research was designed. Following that we look (Chapter 3) at management perspectives on residential child care in our three study authorities. Chapter 4 then discusses different categories of homes and their residents. In Chapter 5 we consider daily life in children's homes. This is followed by a section on staffing (Chapter 6), and Chapter 7 is concerned with the quality of care in homes. We end by summarising some of the main themes in the research and their implications.

Summary points

- This study revisits the scene described in the 1985 report *Children's Homes* and considers how residential child care provided in three local authorities has changed over a decade.

- Over this period, much uncertainty and dissatisfaction has developed nationally over the role and functioning of children's homes. This was exacerbated by a series of widely publicised crises.

- Between 1985 and 1995, the number of young people living in children's homes on any one day more than halved. This is part of a broader international trend.

- A number of positive measures were introduced by government in an attempt to raise standards in children's homes, including major new legislation.

- A wide range of economic and social developments over the 1980s and 1990s are likely to have had an adverse effect on children and adolescents, including increasing the number of children in need.

- Much child care research has been undertaken over the past decade, which provides a better understanding of the experiences of children looked after by local authorities. Included in this are studies showing that residential care is still used extensively, particularly for adolescents. A body of work has also demonstrated that, for comparable groups of young people, children's homes are equally effective in meeting their objectives as their main alternatives, especially foster care.

2

Design of the Research

Sociologists have long taken an interest in sensitive topics and our research would certainly fall into this category (Renzetti and Lee 1993). On the fieldwork visit to the first of our sample of homes, the researcher, who was expected, was asked to provide evidence of identity before being allowed admission. It was feared by the staff member concerned that journalists were seeking entry and, indeed, following certain incidents which we detail later, photographers had surreptitiously gained access to the outside of the building and attempted to picture residents through the lounge and kitchen windows.

In-depth studies of children's homes must be among the most sensitive and potentially threatening areas of social inquiry. Lee (1993) has argued that investigations are likely to have major implications for the researched and researchers alike where they meet one of three criteria: if they deal with private and stressful issues; when they study deviancy or social control; and where the emerging information may be stigmatising or incriminating in some way. Our study, and much other research involving children in need, concerns all three components. There are also strong national and local political dimensions, adding further sensitivity, as elected representatives are ultimately responsible for running most homes. Furthermore, neighbours may be unsympathetic or hostile, particularly if property has been stolen or damaged. In addition, the lifestyles of some young people may lead to reproach. The physical and sexual abuse of young people brings additional concern. In this context, staff will be eager to convince researchers and the wider public that they are acting professionally.

Hence our research was likely to be highly sensitive and we considered carefully its design and execution. This chapter outlines our approach to the study – why certain areas were selected for exploration and the specific methods felt to be most appropriate.

Theory and concepts

At one level, certain decisions were self-evident as the comparative nature of the study meant that similar issues were to be explored as in 1985. A degree of consistency, therefore, was important, although new developments gave rise to specific questions. As with the original publication, we wanted to map the occupancy of children's homes and the circumstances by which young people arrived there. This led to questions about the relationship between children's homes and the wider child welfare system. We also set out to explore whether there were distinctive organisational styles of home and the implications of this. This included examining the objectives of homes and how these were pursued. The regimes adopted were thus analysed, including how staff roles were allocated; how homes were actually run on a daily basis; patterns of interaction between staff and residents; how control was established; and links with family, community and other relevant professionals. We have a special interest in young people's education and have also been undertaking a sub-study of this area (Berridge and Brodie 1996). Throughout the project we tried to be alert to the experiences of children who may be particularly disadvantaged, including those from minority ethnic groups, girls and disabled children (Eichler 1988).

As said already, this study is more evaluative than its predecessor and has been approached by using a range of complementary methods. On the one hand, as before, we sought the perspectives of a range of participants in children's homes – managers, heads of homes and other staff and young people – about how institutions currently function and their perceived strengths and weaknesses. In addition, however, we investigated independently and in detail key components that we felt were essential in understanding the quality of care offered by homes.

By now readers should have gleaned some insights into our particular approach to researching children's homes and it is necessary to make this theoretical framework more explicit. As with other disciplines perhaps, sociologists seem happiest when disagreeing among themselves and there are long-standing philosophical disputes about which forms of analysis provide the most fruitful or legitimate means of understanding the social world. Perhaps the most common polarisation is that between, on the one hand, *positivist* approaches which tend to adopt a broad macro stance and are interested in social structures and social facts. These use quantitative methods to test hypotheses and usually strive for statistical reliability. This is often contrasted with a more *interpretive* approach, which focuses on micro interaction and the meanings to the actors involved. Qualitative methods tend to be used to generate hypotheses rather than test them (Silverman 1993).

Our position on these matters is in line with Layder's (1993) analysis, which asserted that neither of these two approaches is sufficient in itself. Individual interactions and perspectives can only be fully understood in the social contexts within which they occur. Similarly, broad analyses can operate at such a level of generality as to leave much unexplained. Instead Layder has outlined a 'realist' approach which he defines as follows:

> The realist model of social science has been developed as an alternative to the conventional positivist notion. Put very simply, a central feature of realism is its

attempt to preserve a 'scientific' attitude towards social analysis at the same time as recognising the importance of actors' meanings and in some way incorporating them in research. (p.16)

This model operates at four main levels, which can be seen to be relevant to our study of children's homes: first, there is the overall societal *context* and its main institutions (such as the legal framework and status of residential child care); second, the specific *setting* (for example, individual children's homes and neighbourhoods); third *situated activity* (daily interactions in homes); and finally *self* (children's individual characteristics and prior experiences). Two further elements are important to the model, namely *history* and *power*. As revealed in the opening chapter, this set of institutions cannot be fully understood without reference to their long-term and more recent past. Indeed, our study focuses in detail on developments over the last ten years. In addition, concerning *power*, the child welfare service has important social control functions (Parton 1991), while maintaining order within children's homes will emerge as a key theme in later chapters. While these are the main constituent parts of Layder's model, not all will necessarily receive equal attention in individual studies.

Thus quantitative and qualitative data are used in a complementary fashion to provide insight into structural factors as well as individual interactions and behaviours. This approach is not without its difficulties and it should not be confused with indiscriminate eclecticism or a restricted 'crosstabs and case studies' mentality (Brannen 1992). In contrast, we feel that this strategy is a helpful way of undertaking applied social research and understanding such a complex set of institutions as children's homes as well as, perhaps, to making some contribution towards their improvement. It is consistent with the 'methodological pluralism' advocated by Cheetham and her colleagues (1992) as well as to a value-position that believes that the disadvantaged should have opportunities to express their views (Berridge 1995a). An advantage of this approach in child care research is that it enables one to link processes with outcomes: it seems insufficient to identify outcomes if one is not really clear what they are outcomes *of*.

Selecting the current sample

It is important to explain how our current sample of homes was identified. We worked with the same three English local authorities as previously. One is an urban authority in the north ('North'); the second an inner London borough with a diverse ethnic population ('Borough'); and the third is a predominantly rural county in the south ('South'). In our original study, the sample of 20 homes included 14 local authority-managed establishments: the three authorities contributed respectively five, six and three homes in line with their overall residential child care populations. In addition, our earlier work examined three voluntary homes and three private facilities used by South. These 20 establishments were mainstream, on the whole small children's homes rather than larger specialist resources such as community homes with education (CHEs) homes with observation and assessment facilities (O & As) or secure units, which were felt to be quite different forms of provision and raised specific issues. Interestingly, these more specialist resources had also previously attracted significant research attention, whereas the more general children's homes, despite their numerical predominance, had been largely overlooked (Bullock, Little and Millham 1993a). In fact the 1985 study was one of the first broad-based empirical studies of this sector.

Our intention on this occasion was to revisit this sample of homes ten years later and to substitute those that had closed with others that reflected current patterns of use. The next chapter, drawing on interviews with managers, sets out in greater detail developments in the three authorities over the decade, including how and why particular decisions had been made. However, an important early finding is that, of the 20 homes operational in 1985, only *four* were still open after ten years. All six voluntary and private homes had closed, as had 10 of the 14 local authority facilities. Furthermore, two of the four homes that were still open were due for imminent closure: one consisted of a large, inappropriate and neglected building, while the other was located in a high crime and very unsafe area. As we shall see, community integration can have its disadvantages as well as benefits, and for these two homes the major control problems stemmed not so much from residents going out but in preventing outsiders from breaking in.

The degree of discontinuity was uneven among the three authorities. In North, for example, three of the five original homes were still in existence. In Borough, in contrast, it had been planned during the early stages of our research that two of the original six homes would continue with revised, authority-wide functions and be joined in this by a third new home. However, due to a financial crisis it was subsequently decided that the borough would not be able to proceed with any of these facilities and, instead, would use exclusively private sector homes.

It is apparent that the residential sector in these three areas had experienced considerable change, a strong theme that emerges throughout this report. Yet we know it is important to provide continuity and predictability for children in public care given that this is a feature of their lives that has generally been lacking (Kahan 1994). There is also evidence that homes deliver better quality care where they have not recently experienced reorganisation leading to a major change in function (Sinclair and Gibbs 1996). Incidentally, this lack of continuity is reflected in the fact that, of the 136 staff working in the 20 homes in the early 1980s, only four (3 per cent) were still residential child care workers in the same agencies ten years on (see also Chapter 6.) Transfer between occupations, of course, is not uncommon. Some may be residential workers elsewhere or involved with different client groups. It is also known that a small number at least had trained as fieldworkers. In what is still predominantly a female workforce, no doubt a number of the earlier sample are combining work with child care responsibilities of their own. However, these figures do not suggest that staff resources are being harnessed or that there has been much of a career structure for residential workers. We need to know much more about this subject (Millham, Bullock and Hosie 1980). As will be revealed in the following chapter, discontinuity was also evident in management.

Our current sample of children's homes included all residential units managed by North and South. The situation was more complex with Borough and the private sector. We decided to replace the three planned London homes with the three private facilities used most frequently by the borough. Two of these were part of groups in London and the south-east and were eager to participate. The third proved to be more elusive, even despite strong encouragement by the local authority. The first we approached closed down the day before our visit – hopefully the two events were unconnected! The borough had to find alternative placements for five of its children without prior notice. The second, following a positive meeting but irritating delay, declined our request for involvement as the proprietor was spending a significant amount of time abroad. The third on our list was unenthusiastic from the outset and also seemed unsure whether it needed permission to participate from the authority (which was its most frequent user) or the local inspection unit. It came as no great surprise when our request was declined, although we were disappointed as by then our interest had been stimulated by the sight of a newish Rolls Royce parked ostentatiously outside the front of the building, which did little to allay stereotypes about the private sector. We did not encounter such extravagance in the other private homes.

By now our trudge around the south-east and forced intimacy with the A to Z meant that our enthusiasm was waning and we decided to abandon our search for a further private sector home. However, the impact of this was alleviated as a third independent facility was included in our sample, having been used regularly by South and being considered almost part of its own resources. This experience with the private homes raise issues about openness and accountability. It has important implications for researchers as the private sector grows. It is impossible to predict what influence this process has had on our final sample of homes, although it is likely that the ones that participated were more confident about what they had to offer than those which declined. However, what this has taught us is that there is considerable variation among private sector (and local authority) facilities. We should also remind ourselves that probably not all local authority homes would take part voluntarily if they were not under pressure to do so from management.

There is a further important issue we need to raise concerning sample selection, namely that our final group of homes included two that cater specifically for children with severe learning disabilities and additional health needs. We are unaware of other current studies of children's homes that include this group and our reasoning was as follows. The Children Act 1989 includes disabled children, and services to support them, as part of mainstream legislation and we felt we would be unjustified in excluding this group. It could be argued that to do otherwise would be discriminatory. Indeed, local authority homes that cater for disabled children are governed by the Children's Homes Regulations (Department of Health 1991b). Admittedly this area raises specific issues and services tend to be organised in a particular way, but as a society we also have choices about how we structure services for children in need who are not disabled and we could follow a similar line if we wished. About a quarter of all homes now cater for children with learning, physical and/or sensory impairments (but not necessarily exclusively), and so it is a significant part of overall provision (Department of Health 1996b, table G). When we paid initial visits to our participating local authorities and asked what children's homes currently existed, in both Borough and North reference was spontaneously made by managers to the two facilities in question: South did not have such an establishment. The two acknowledged that these homes were not as fully integrated as they might be with other residential services but, nevertheless, saw them as important local facilities.

An additional reason for including these two homes, consistent with the overall framework outlined earlier in this chapter, is that questioning traditional classifications helps to develop concepts and insights into an area. In relation to policy and practice, it might also be that different forms of provision have particular approaches or strengths that can be shared across services. For example, as we shall see, when Borough closed all of its own children's homes it maintained the facility for disabled children. Residential care seems to be more appreciated for disabled children and parents more powerful in ensuring its delivery. There are some interesting parallels and contrasts in our data which we develop in the following chapters.

Admittedly the 1985 study did not include services specifically for disabled children and their families (although at the time the two services in question did not then exist). There was a tendency then to keep matters conceptually and administratively separate, which is now changing. As we shall see, including this group poses complexities analytically but we feel there are clear theoretical, policy and practice benefits for the research.

Table 2.1 summarises the 1995 and 1985 research samples. Due to the general overall decline in the number of children's homes, we now have 12 homes rather than the original 20. More local authorities would have had to be included to broaden the sample, which would have been inconsistent with the follow-up approach. Hence we have studied in detail seven local authority homes, an additional two which cater specifically for children with severe learning

Table 2.1 1995 and 1985 research samples compared

Sector	1995	1985
Local authority homes	9	14
(children with severe learning disabilities)	(2)	–
Private homes	3	3
Voluntary homes	–	3
TOTAL	12	20

disabilities and three private homes. The authorities concerned did not make significant use of voluntary residential facilities, which we are aware varies regionally. The voluntary sector makes a major contribution to child care in the UK and has often developed innovatory models of service delivery in place of traditional residential approaches. Yet, especially in light of the considerable difficulties in residential care outlined in our opening chapter, it is a pity that the major children's charities in particular, given their long expertise, have not demonstrated more interest in this field.

We do not claim that our sample is necessarily representative of the wider scene, although it portrays the residential options available for children in three contrasting English authorities and therefore cannot be lightly dismissed. The original study was felt to be consistent with the broader picture (Department of Health 1991a) and we would be surprised if the current portrayal is totally idiosyncratic.

Research methods

As explained earlier, a variety of complementary methods was used for data collection. The most important resource in any study is the researchers themselves and a colleague was recruited specifically for this work. Though she undertook the bulk of the fieldwork visits to the 12 homes, all research tasks were shared and this provided a necessary form of validation. As an important element of the researcher's responsibilities was to visit children's homes at length and observe, interact and talk with young people, we thought that the best people to test in advance for these skills were young people themselves. Therefore, we worked with a group of residents from a local children's home, who played a formal role in the recruitment process by separately interviewing candidates for the research assistant post (Berridge and Wenman 1995). This worked remarkably well and, fortunately, the young people's preference matched the results of academic assessments. We believe the Warner Report recommendations on recruiting residential staff could go further in this direction, and involving young people more formally might help instil a stronger sense of responsibility and commitment (Department of Health 1992) (see also Townsley and Macadam

888888888

(1996), which discusses the involvement of people with learning difficulties in staff selection). Despite being a positive experience all round, and offering to do virtually all the work, we were nevertheless defeated when it came to trying to get the local authority to extract some positive publicity with local media from the experience. Consequently, as is so often the case elsewhere, so much of what one reads and hears about children's homes concerns crisis and disobedience and the stigma and stereotypes associated with residential care remain undiminished.

The early stages of a research project entail immersion in the relevant academic and professional literature. We also began the lengthy process of gaining access to the three local authorities and 12 homes. Two of the authorities were eager to participate but we were dismayed to receive a curt rejection letter from the director of social services in the third. Urging reconsideration, and explaining that the study could not proceed at all if only one agency opted out, the decision was reversed: obstinacy can pay off.

We then met with senior managers in each agency who were responsible for children's residential services. Though the design of the study was already broadly in place, we tried to make the research as collaborative as possible. Therefore, we offered to include within reason additional dimensions to the study if these were of particular local concern. We also discussed strategies for dissemination and, as a further means of reciprocating, volunteered our services in making any other local contribution such as a training input or in relation to elected members. Police checks were undertaken by the university at our request on the backgrounds of both researchers and copies issued to managers as well as each of the 12 homes. It is encouraging to note that several homes asked unprompted about this precaution, in marked contrast to the 1980s study. Such checks obviously provide only a minimal protection but should become the norm, we feel, for researchers with significant unsupervised access to children or to case records.

Our identification of the research sample and approaches to the private sector have been described already. We arranged an informal initial visit to each facility where we asked to meet with the head of home and, if possible and separately, wider staff group and residents. The purpose of our research and methods were outlined, including the subsequent visits to the homes. Explaining what research entails is not straightforward and one female resident asked unkindly what were our real jobs. We had prepared in advance for staff and children separate leaflets with accompanying photographs summarising our research. This was a useful measure and had a significant impact on the children in particular, a number of whom remarkably kept the leaflet over several months while others referred to its contents. We stated that we were undertaking the study in order to let it be known more widely what children's homes were really like and to try to identify ways in which they might be improved. It was added that, when we subsequently visited homes, we would withdraw from a situation if asked to do so by a member of staff or resident, for example if someone became out of control or distressed. We commented that we spent much time visiting children's homes and were aware that such circumstances might arise. Staff especially seemed to appreciate this suggestion. In fact there were no occasions on which we were asked to withdraw, although we voluntarily moved to adjoining rooms on two occasions: once when a girl became violent and again when staff were becoming visibly very anxious. There were also two occasions when we were asked not to attend parts of staff meetings. Overall, however, staff said they were pleased to be able to share with us the difficulties of the work as well as its rewards.

Generally, our perception is that the approach to gaining access worked well and we tried to be conscious of the interpersonal skills that can help put people at ease. There were probably two areas which did not proceed so smoothly. First, about a third of our homes were very difficult to contact and did not respond to our letters or phone messages. If they are behaving similarly to parents or other professionals this will appear inefficient and unprofessional as well as disrespectful. Second, in about the same proportion of homes, though not necessarily the same ones, despite our elaborate advance preparations, staff said they had not been expecting us when we arrived for our fieldwork visit. In fact residents seemed better informed than were staff. This indicated that communication in several homes was poor and we hope they do better when new residents arrive, where feelings of intrusion and rejection will already be acute. Nevertheless, the vast majority of staff and residents subsequently made us very welcome when we visited homes.

Specific sources of information were as follows.

Managers

As part of the process of gaining access, we met at the outset senior managers in the three local authorities with responsibility for children's homes. This gave us a general idea of the context and any particular local issues of which we needed to be aware. In addition, we held more formal interviews with managers at the conclusion of our work in the authorities. In each of the three cases, two managers were involved: one who answered questions about current services and a colleague who addressed developments over the previous decade. These interviews were semi-structured and would fall into the 'long interview' category (McCracken 1988). This concerns not only duration but also the flexibility with which key informants can range across what they feel to be pertinent topics. Similar interviews were held with the proprietors of the three private homes, where we also touched on issues specifically relevant to the independent sector such as relationships with local authorities.

Participant observation

However, the main method used to gather information on our 12 homes was participant observation and in 1995 one of us visited each home intensively for four or five days. In contrast to the 1980s study, in which the researcher physically lived in each home, on this occasion we were able to stay overnight at only 3 of the 12. This is largely attributable to the absence of accommodation, which is linked to patterns of staff residence. Indeed, in the 1980s all but 2 of the 20 heads of homes lived permanently at the homes, as did a quarter of other staff in local authority homes. This rose to half of all staff in the voluntary homes in the original sample and virtually all those working in the private sector. On this occasion, however, *none* of the 103 staff lived in. This is a major shift and is in marked contrast to the therapeutic communities, where staff residence is still common, if not preferred (Little 1995). An important change has therefore occurred in the *meaning* of residential care for the staff concerned. The vocational element has thus diminished and fewer of staffs' own needs, such as housing, are met by entering the work. Though the lack of space seemed to have been the main reason, there was also a perception that it may not have been considered appropriate for us to 'live in', particularly for the male researcher.

There have been a number of classic participation studies in American sociology including jazz musicians and drug users (Becker 1963), pool-room 'hustlers' (Polsky 1967) and the rather challenging participant investigation of homosexual activity in men's public lavatories (Humphreys 1970). Participation as a method has been selected in our study as it enables the researcher to enter into the social world of staff and residents and describe and analyse as accurately as possible how these institutions function. As we shall see, there is also sometimes a contrast between what managers and staff say is occurring and what actually happens.

The general term 'participant observation' has a variety of meanings. Our approach is not easily categorised according to the common four-fold typology of complete participant, participant as observer, observer as participant or complete observer, but would be a combination of the second and third types. The complication arises probably because children as a social category adds a complex dimension and we were in fact studying not one social group but two – staff also (see Gans 1982).

Marshall and Rossman's (1995) approach to designing qualitative research is perhaps more fruitful in helping to understand our roles as participants. On their first criterion, our *degree of 'participantness'* was that we tried to take part as much as possible in the life of the homes, including meals, activities and any outings. However, we made it clear that we were not temporary members of staff and, apart from extreme circumstances – such as to avoid accidents or physical injury – did not wish to exert adult authority. Second, regarding degree of '*revealedness*', we were open about the fact that we were researchers, that we were visiting 12 homes nationally and would be writing a report based on the experience. Though we gave a broad indication of our areas of interest, we did not divulge in detail what these were.

A third consideration is *level of intensity* and we visited each home from early morning to late at night over the four or five days. Staff and residents were often surprised that we were not following 'shifts'. Though our impression of homes is a snapshot and still no doubt relatively superficial, carers and children did seem to appreciate the fact that we were prepared to take a close look at their worlds and problems.

A final dimension of qualitative research identified by Marshall and Rossman is whether the focus is *specific* or *diffuse*. Here we had particular areas of interest and, of course, were interested in comparisons with residential services a decade earlier. Yet, consistent with the overall framework outlined previously, we also wanted to retain sufficient flexibility so that we could be alert to major issues identified by staff and children. In addition, it is probably helpful to think of us during our participant visits as occupying the role of 'friends' to residents and staff rather than supervisor, leader or observer (Fine and Sandstrom 1988).

There were several sources of data during these fieldwork visits. We interviewed heads of homes as early as we could during the stay, which consisted of the 'long interview' format as with managers (McCracken 1988). Semi-structured interviews were also held with a range of staff and, less formally, with children who were prepared to talk. Questionnaires were designed to record standardised biographical information on residents. We sometimes completed these ourselves from files but more commonly did so in association with the head of home or a senior colleague. This certainly saved time. However, it was also encouraging to discover that staff were often concerned about the implications of giving relative strangers access to children's records, whereas in the 1980s study there was very little, if any, inhibition. Brief questionnaires were also given to staff to enable us to form a comparative profile of their characteristics.

The appeal of the participant observation method is that it gives rise to a vast richness of qualitative data on everyday occurrences, interactions and problems. Once again we tried to be consistent with the 1985 *Children's Homes* study and to discern different styles of home. We were interested to see whether the information that managers, heads of homes and staff gave was operationalised, such as objectives for homes and specific methods of work. We explored everyday life in homes, including staff–child interaction, methods of control and how staff occupied their time. Evidence of links with families, schools, neighbourhoods and wider professionals was also sought. The format of this qualitative data was structured in advance in the form of participant observation schedules. Detailed notes and quotations were written during the day at grabbed opportunities or in contrived visits to the toilet: more than one child asked after our health. Our quantitative data were analysed using SPSS and Microsoft Excel software packages. Established approaches to qualitative analysis were adopted, comprising descriptions and classifications leading to connections and the identification of common themes (Dey 1993; Glaser 1978; Glaser and Strauss 1967; Silverman 1993).

This outline of participant observation in children's homes hopefully has a certain planned coherence, but the execution is rather more problematic. There are decisions to be made about what to wear, what to carry, where to sit and how to behave. Trust and relationships have to be established and maintained, but not to the degree that children become inappropriately dependent, which is a danger with those who yearn for affection. Departure needs to be carefully planned. Sexualised displays by children have to be discouraged and an appropriate response given when asked to read a bedtime story, go to look at something in a bedroom or when a child asks to sit on your lap. There are difficult decisions about whether to intervene and glimpses of cruelty and deep unhappiness can be unsettling. Issues of safety and vulnerability can also arise for the researchers. The number of grey hairs increased as the fieldwork progressed.

Social research raises important ethical considerations regarding obligations to society, funders and employers, colleagues and research participants (Social Research Association 1994). Studies in children's homes pose specific issues which researchers need to consider carefully (Alderson 1995). We provided the customary guarantees to staff and residents of anonymity and confidentiality, but not if evidence emerged that a child was at risk of serious harm, where we confirmed that we would take action (no such cases arose). We made it clear that no young person or member of staff had to talk to us if they did not wish to do so. This was done particularly with children in mind, although we appreciate that empowering young people in the context of an otherwise unequal relationship is problematic. In addition, we attempted to provide all research participants with detailed information about the research and, within obvious constraints, shall try to do as best we can regarding its conclusions.

Quality of care

The research was completed according to plan, with one exception. In seeking to investigate the outcomes of interventions, that is, the impact on residents of living in a children's home, we decided to use the Assessment and Action Records of the Department of Health's (1995b) *Looking After Children* planning and monitoring package (see also Parker *et al.* 1991). These consist of a series of age-related tools, which enable children's progress to be monitored across a range of key developmental areas, largely by concentrating on the quality of parenting provided. Our intention was for the records to be used by staff and young people, in association with social workers where appropriate, at six-monthly intervals. We started with the local authority homes but, despite our strenuous efforts, we were unable to get many of even the initial round of forms completed.

The reasons for this were complex. A major factor was that we were working with the Records at their pilot stage and, at the time, the authorities had not yet made a central commitment to implementing the package throughout their service. We were therefore operating in a vacuum and individual residential homes were probably not the best place to start. Some homes did manage to complete many forms but we were informed that young people frequently refused to co-operate. Similar points emerged in a national evaluation of the piloting of the *Looking After Children* initiative, which emphasised the importance of developing a strong culture of monitoring and evaluation. It also found problems in implementing the package in parts of the residential sector (Ward 1995). However, as we shall see, we suspect that inability to complete this task is linked to wider questions about the functioning of parts of the residential sector (see also Chapter 7).

Yet even if our original strategy had worked to plan there would have been limitations in the data that emerged. For example, the Assessment and Action Records are not written specifically with children with severe learning disabilities in mind. Furthermore, as we shall see, because of the nature of residential services for this group, the small size of most of the 12 homes in our sample and the often transitory nature of residence, our follow-up groups would have been very small and restricted to about a third of the original number.

Instead, therefore, we modified our approach to evaluation and shifted our focus away from outcomes for individual children to the quality of care provided by homes. We developed what we termed an 'Institutional Variables Summary', which contained quantitative data adapted from our interviews and periods of participant observation in each home. This was developed into a quality of care index for each establishment and, when other data were taken into account relating to child and staff characteristics and structural features of homes, statistical analysis was undertaken in order to identify the main factors associated with what we defined as high quality care. We return to this in more detail in Chapter 7.

Having explained how our research was designed, let us now turn to the results.

Summary points

- The current research sample comprises 12 homes: 9 are managed by local authorities, including 2 specifically for children with severe learning disabilities, and 3 are private homes.

- The study uses a complementary quantitative and qualitative approach, which is felt to have advantages in undertaking applied policy-related research.

- The main research method used to study the 12 establishments was participant observation, in which features of the homes were systematically analysed. Biographical data were gathered on residents and staff. Interviews were conducted with managers, heads of homes, staff and young people. We analysed the quality of care offered by homes and linked this to organisational, staffing and child characteristics.

- Only 4 of the original sample of 20 homes were in existence 10 years later.

- Barely 4 of the 136 staff in the 1985 study were still residential child care workers with the same employer on this occasion.

- Again in marked contrast to the situation in 1985, none of the staff also lived at the residential home in the current study.

3

Managers' Perspectives

The management of children's homes has been identified as a key factor in delivering effective services (Department of Health 1991b; Kahan 1994). Indeed, in many of the recent crises in residential settings, deficiencies in external management have been pinpointed as a significant contributory element (Berridge and Brodie 1996). Hence the longest section of the Utting Report was concerned with management issues (Department of Health 1991a), while the Warner review addressed more of its recommendations to management than elsewhere (Department of Health 1992). In view of this, it is surprising that researchers have paid little attention to the management of residential child care. None of the 100 or so studies included in the Dartington review of research on residential care appear to have management as a focus (Bullock *et al.* 1993a). Much earlier work portrayed residential care as rather self-contained, which of course many of the larger institutions actually were (Millham, Bullock and Cherrett 1979). More recent studies investigate establishments in their wider professional and social contexts, yet the external management dimension is usually absent. It is therefore encouraging that work has commenced specifically on this topic at the Cardiff Business School.

The term 'management' obviously embodies a variety of meanings, including planning, maintaining standards and resourcing. Similarly, a range of individuals exercise management functions. In a later chapter we consider the perspectives of heads of homes as managers. However, here we are concerned with senior managers in the three local authorities with responsibilities for overseeing residential services. This dimension, we feel, is important in order to discern developments in residential and other child care services over the past decade. As we shall see, there have been a number of policy, organisational and financial influences on children's homes that are important in understanding their current functioning.

We therefore interviewed two senior managers in each of our three local authorities: one with current responsibility for children's homes and another who was well positioned to provide information about developments over the last ten years. These representatives were mostly third or second tier and proved to be a detailed and refreshingly frank source of information. Interviews usually took most of an afternoon and we were grateful for this amount of time from such busy individuals. We focused on the main themes covered in other parts of our research, including changes over the previous decade and their perceived causes and effects; management structure and support; and professional and community links. Managers' offices yielded interesting insights into their roles and priorities, ranging from the hectic disorder in one section with frequent interruptions and requests for information, to a more serene reflection possible elsewhere. The contents of bookshelves also symbolised some current dilemmas, where it was noticed that imposing manuals on *Total Quality Management, Business Principles for Purchasers* and the like vied for space with Department of Health guidance and the more traditional Bowlby, Goffman and other social work texts.

A decade of residential child care

Major changes had clearly occurred in the residential sectors of each of our three authorities and we saw in the last chapter that only 4 of the 20 homes from the 1985 study were still open. We deal with Borough shortly. In both North and South, the number of residential places (or still, colloquially, 'beds') had been reduced by three-quarters – slightly more than the national trend. Apart from its smaller homes, the latter originally had no fewer than three community homes with education (CHEs) and another with observation and assessment (O & A) within its boundaries, each of which had now closed. Thus the larger institutions in both areas had disappeared. A manager in North observed, with a certain irony, that matters have in fact turned full circle not once but twice since she entered social work: the authority began in the 1960s with large campus-style homes, which it transformed in the 1970s into smaller, more personal, 'family-style' units. Then in the 1980s larger, multi-purpose units became more fashionable, which have now been replaced with small facilities. She hoped to have retired before the next round.

As discussed later, homes in North had developed more specialist functions whereas in South this had been problematic. We were also interested in the location of establishments and whether now, for example, homes were more likely to be based in communities rather than physically and socially separate. Managers in both North and South stressed that they would not feel able to open new facilities in neighbourhoods due to local opposition – they thus had no influence over their location, which presented serious difficulties. Changes in the pattern of residential services had arisen due to closures and relocation to existing premises. One manager observed wistfully, 'it's all historical plant'.

Various reasons were proposed in North and South for these policy changes which concerned professional, organisational and financial factors. Particularly in North, there was a desire to develop alternatives to residential care, such as an increase in adolescent fostering, and a sense that residence should become very much a last resort. The authority had developed a positive youth justice policy, including, for example, bail support, which successfully managed to avoid significant use of custody. Similar thinking was being applied to services for children in need more generally. There was also an organisational dimension to the developments, and consultation and communication were reported to be poor between care managers (purchasers) and service managers (providers) about the exact nature of proposed changes. As a consequence, confidence was lost and the out-of-borough placement budget tripled in a short period, requiring drastic remedies.

In South, the closure of residential homes was said to be essentially finance-led. There was an element of recycling resources in order to diversify services, such as to develop family centres and other preventive approaches and also to support professional fostering. In addition, the former approved schools were felt to be no longer appropriate and there was a desire to move children into mainstream schools. However, our interviewee – whose responsibilities ranged across children's services and would not appear, therefore, to have vested interests – argued that management was prejudiced against residential care and closures seemed to offer short-term opportunities to generate resources.

Managers interviewed in Borough, whose responsibilities also ranged across children's services, were equally critical of developments. In general, it was acknowledged that the quality of care provided in the late 1980s in the authority's own residential homes was often insufficient and staff morale was low. Much effort was put into tackling this, associated with, and facilitated by, the introduction of the Children Act 1989 in 1991 onwards. Borough has retained throughout a facility offering short-term breaks for children with severe learning disabilities, which we scrutinise later. It was eventually decided that the remainder of Borough's own residential provision would be concentrated in three children's resource centres – two for adolescents and another for those who were younger. Staff in these would be professionally qualified and would also act as case managers, holding overall social work responsibility. The centres would undertake mainly crisis reception and assessment functions. The intention would be for young people to stay no more than three months and, if longer-term residential care were required, a placement in a private or voluntary facility would be sought.

However, shortly before they were due to be introduced, these plans were shelved due to a financial crisis in Borough. In real terms, there was a reduction in the overall social services budget of some £2.5 million, followed by another £500,000 the following year. Children and family services bore the brunt of these cuts and were disproportionately affected, an interesting departure from what more often seems to have been the case in the past where they have been protected. Thus elected members decided that Borough would no longer retain this residential care and all children requiring this service would instead be placed in private or voluntary facilities. Interestingly, as also occurred in Warwickshire (Cliffe with Berridge 1991), this did not apply to the unit catering for disabled children, although a variety of options were being explored, including transfer of its management to the voluntary sector. When asked to explain this apparent inconsistency on the part of elected members, managers suggested that the local political ramifications of closing the unit could be quite considerable as parents would not tolerate it. Disability, being cross-class, thus attracts different services. We return to this later.

Borough managers were strongly critical of the general policy (for non-disabled children) on two main grounds: financial and in relation to quality of care. Regarding the former, comparative costing of child care services is a complex matter and one needs to be careful that exact comparisons are being made (Knapp and Robertson 1989). Nonetheless, it was maintained that, since the policy had been introduced, using exclusively independent sector homes had actually led to an overall *increase* rather than reduction in budget. However, this is difficult to confirm from independent published statistics (Chartered Institute of Public Finance and Accountancy 1996). (Incidentally, Warwickshire, which was the first local authority nationally to pursue a similar policy, did not find that using the private sector was cheaper than running its own residential resources, nor did it set out with savings in mind (Cliffe with Berridge 1991).) Managers in Borough argued that they were at the behest of the market and, ultimately, would have no choice but to pay what was demanded. It was alleged that some proprietors had begun to act as cartels and form agreements on charges, not quite how markets in social care are supposed to perform. Interestingly, the expression 'it's a providers' market' arose on a number of occasions during our study.

Moreover, there were concerns about the quality of care provided to Borough children. Managers were clear that private homes often provided good quality care and developed beneficial partnerships with the authority. Two such homes are probably represented in our research sample. However, there were strong concerns about the way in which parts of the sector operated. For example, most homes were outside London and sometimes quite a long distance away. They could be in isolated rural areas, which posed problems in maintaining contacts with families and on eventual return. Some of the children involved were also quite young. Furthermore, many of them were from minority ethnic groups and they could be placed in predominantly or exclusively white areas: this is inconsistent with Section 22(5)(c) of the Children Act 1989. Similar concerns were raised in a recent small-scale study of independent fostering agencies (Department of Health Social Services Inspectorate 1995a).

Borough managers found it difficult to monitor practices in private homes. This is understandable given the fact that, at the time of our interview, there were over 210 children from the authority living in no fewer than 70 private establishments. The safety of children, therefore, could be jeopardised. 'Drift' in placements was also a worry (Rowe and Lambert 1973), in which the distance and dispersion might make it difficult for planning to be sufficiently proactive. There could indeed be some homes in which the survival of the business depended on the retention of children. Problems in monitoring also existed in relation to small, unregistered children's homes (Department of Health Social Services Inspectorate 1994b): Borough had the policy of not using such establishments but managers would not always be aware, for example, if children were transferred between premises within the same group. Furthermore, education colleagues in Borough were critical of the educational experiences provided by some private homes. Host local education authorities and mainstream schools often did not welcome problematic pupils descending from the London boroughs. There is also research evidence that racism is more likely to occur in predominantly white schools (Troyna and Hatcher 1992).

In addition to these general changes in our three local authorities, we inquired why specific decisions had been taken to close homes that featured in our original 1985 study – why some rather than others? In one authority, a manager remarked that there was no logic in the closure decisions and specific reasons, therefore, were difficult to discern. Another manager remarked that the closure *process*, that is, the way in which it was actually managed, was 'appalling'. These, then, were minority views, although whether the staff involved would agree might of course be a different matter. When pursued in some detail, we were able to obtain explanations for 12 of the 16 closures from our 1985 sample. Naturally, several reasons might be involved. However, half of the closures seem to have occurred essentially because the model and/or methods of care provided were considered to be no longer appropriate. One had become a family centre which, interestingly, maintained a small amount of residential accommodation for families. Another was managed by a national voluntary agency which had changed the direction of its work: the original home now comprised a community facility for youths together with family support. Two more of the original homes were based on the 'family group-style approach', one of which the first time round did not feel particularly welcoming. The other home in this group was described in the 1985 study as, '…part of a home which was organised as a series of cottages, popular during the inter-war period, which sheltered in its heyday upwards of 500 children' (p.68). The campus was subsequently sold to become expensive private housing: exclusive accommodation once again but with a rather different social profile to its original inhabitants.

The other six closures fell equally into three categories. Two were voluntary homes that had ceased to be used by the host authority purely to make financial savings. The authority had residential care of its own, which would be maintained as a priority. One of these voluntary homes, overall, was certainly among the most impressive of the original group of 20 – in terms of physical environment, quality of care and children's perceptions – yet was among the earliest to close.

Managers explained that another two homes had discontinued largely because of the unsuitable premises in which they were located. One was in a dilapidated condition and required considerable structural work and therefore expense. The other, which was relatively new, was poorly designed and aspects of its layout were unsafe.

The final two homes had closed specifically because there was dissatisfaction about the quality of care they provided. It was felt that one home had never really functioned as intended and it was alleged that there were concerns over some relationships that had developed. In the other, allegations concerned financial impropriety and that aspects of children's physical care had been neglected. With these two exceptions, perhaps, we were not informed of any other institutionalised malpractices, though one in six is hardly reassuring.

The current context

Managers were asked a series of general questions about their departments and the situation of children's homes within them. In response, each of the three authorities was described as being 'purchaser–provider' under different guises, encompassing all client groups. On the provider side, one had a dedicated assistant director responsible for children and family services, but in the other two, a service manager at third tier was the most senior specialist. With regard to residential child care, Borough managers reiterated that – apart from the facility for disabled children – they were exclusively purchasers. Of the two other authorities, only South planned to take its organisational arrangements to the extreme position of entirely delegating budgets. Thus its children's homes, or 'provider units' as they were alluringly termed, would charge fees to purchasers ('care managers', formerly social workers) and if the latter decided not to buy the services of a facility it would close.

As we have already seen, managers interviewed expressed different views over these developments. A minority view was that it was the best way to raise standards, which had been unsuccessful using other methods. The main concern, however, was the division it created within the department: 'It was totally bloody mayhem', as one remarked. A manager in South observed that this was particularly unfortunate given the rift between fieldwork and residential services that has long bedevilled social work (Barclay Committee 1982).

We pursued this theme by asking what were felt to be the benefits and disadvantages of the current local authority management structure for children's homes. One manager was positive in her view that current arrangements had led to a more corporate approach in which children's homes were authority-wide resources and thus accessible by all, compared with a more 'parochial' stance when they were district-based. Apart from this, the other five managers spoke more negatively. In North, the introduction of the purchaser–provider arrangement had seriously hampered professional working relationships, which only after two years were now beginning to be rebuilt. Borough managers were even more disapproving. Following the financial crisis, one of the two assistant director posts would be lost, the number of area offices would be reduced from seven to three and all decisions concerning use of the private and voluntary sectors would be delegated to area managers. Some negotiating of block grants would continue from headquarters but, apart from this, no 'quality control' would be exercised from the centre. The two managers interviewed in Borough thus felt that, as a result of its current policies and structure, the authority would have less control and less quality within what they perceived as a more expensive service. The system would also reinforce the dangerous tendency for social workers to be contented so long as a child was placed, with little monitoring on their part over the quality of care and developments in placements.

In North it was added that children's homes would be likely to receive very little external supervision. Heads of homes reported directly to a service manager, who also had responsibility for family centres and family placement teams. Due to the demands on his time, homes would get little individual attention. There was a strong mutual support group between heads of homes, who met regularly and would often assist one another, but this was an inadequate substitute.

South had pursued a different approach to supporting its children's homes, in which a 'group management' system had been adopted. Group managers were appointed who were responsible for two homes, with an assistant manager located in each. Thus there was no 'head of home' as such. An objective of this approach was to introduce greater flexibility, so that, for example, there would be fewer institutional barriers preventing children or staff spending time in more than one home. The responsibilities of group managers were said to concern negotiating with purchasers, 'business planning' and contributing to the authority-wide policy process. As a result, they initially spent little time actually in homes and this was a factor that was apparent during our period of observations. Subsequently, however, the situation was reported to have improved.

We also explored the role of residential care in departments' child care policies. Paradoxically, the clearest view and most positive endorsement of the potential contribution of residential care emerged in Borough, which had entirely dismantled its own service. Here it was stated, in line with the Utting Report (Department of Health 1991a), that there are specific groups of children for whom children's homes are the most appropriate option at certain stages of their care careers. Sibling groups were mentioned specifically. Elsewhere, there was a more uncertain depiction of the role of residential care in agency policy. One manager conceded that, 'residential care may have something to offer'. Another commented that, in her authority, there was currently no overall strategy for residential care in children and family services, and that a different account would emerge depending on who was being consulted. This no doubt both influences and reflects the status of residential care within an agency. In her authority this was said to be quite low: it stemmed from the attitudes of senior purchasers, who held negative perceptions of residential care in general. A similar view was expressed in North, where it was stated that the service tends not to be seen as a positive resource but mainly to be used for negative reasons when all else has failed.

We inquired specifically whether homes were able to function as set out in their Statements of Purpose. These were introduced by the Children Act 1989 and are intended to be a concise summary of what each establishment is setting out to achieve and the manner in which care is provided (Department of Health 1991b). In North it was felt that homes on the whole were able to function as envisaged; however, in South, Statements generally had not been developed – this was approaching three years after the legislation had required them.

As well as the organisation of services, we were interested in managers' perceptions of whether the group(s) of users of residential care had altered over recent years. Interestingly this received mixed responses. In North there was a clear view that the population served by children's homes had become older and posed more entrenched problems in their behaviour. For Borough, in contrast, the profile was thought to be essentially similar, although what had occurred was that young people had been excluded whom it was felt should never have been in residential care in the first place. Managers in South felt that the residential group was now more concentrated into a problematic core. A major contributory factor here was the lack of alternative specialist residential resources, such as the former CHEs. This was said to have brought about 'a huge shift' within the authority, and the smaller children's homes in the midst of communities were dealing with a population that, a decade earlier, was reported to have been accommodated in CHEs. It was also considered that this policy shift had major implications for local schools, in that this group would now be the responsibility of mainstream education rather than residential schools. Managers in North were similarly pressurised to keep to a minimum use of the independent sector.

We explored further the professional context of children's homes in relation to two specific areas: services for young offenders and foster care. The former attracted very positive responses from managers, who felt that their youth justice teams functioned well. The use of custody could be kept at very low levels and in London in particular there was a variety of partnership projects with voluntary agencies. Also in Borough, managers volunteered the information that very positive links had been developed with youth courts and the police. However, the situation was more mixed with foster care. In South fostering was described as a 'major problem' and there were serious difficulties regarding availability and supply. The position was more positive elsewhere, where specialist fostering projects were said to be better established. Nonetheless, providing family placements for adolescents remained a problem. Interestingly, in Borough the major difficulty now was reported to be in recruiting *white* foster carers, whereas in the past the shortage has usually concerned minority ethnic families.

Finally in this section, we asked some questions about quality of care for particular populations and how this was perceived to have been affected by the changes already described. We began with children and families from minority ethnic groups. Two of our three authorities had very small minority populations and it was reported to be unusual for black or Asian children to be admitted to residence. In these areas, managers felt that little had been done to promote cultural awareness or anti-racism. A manager in North described that the services of specialist workers had been bought in on occasions, for example, a Chinese social worker. There was, therefore, slightly greater awareness but, overall, this subject was very much underdeveloped. In Borough, which has a large African-Caribbean population, it was felt that services for this group had deteriorated following the shift to the private sector. This issue had not been considered politically by elected members when the decisions were being made. Consequently, most children from minority ethnic groups living in residential care were placed outside London. They were located in predominantly white areas and contact with parents, family, friends and the black community could be problematic. Managers also commented that this could pose educational risks in inexperienced or unsympathetic schools, as research reveals that African-Caribbean males underachieve educationally and are disproportionately affected by school exclusion (Bourne, Bridges and Searle 1994).

Girls are another group who can present particular needs in residential care, especially where abuse and exploitation have been features of their lives. One interviewee remarked that the movement away from gender segregation that was common in the larger homes has been a positive development and there are also now more women managers in homes. With this exception, it was not felt that residential homes have made much progress in meeting the special needs of girls. Some homes were described as being quite masculine in their ethos, especially where male (delinquent) residents were in a clear majority. North was felt to suffer from a regional sexist culture, which pervaded its residential homes. It was commented in Borough that the private sector caters insufficiently for difficult girls and, since closing its own facilities, placing them has been complex.

Managers were also asked about services for disabled children. South had developed family-based short-term breaks over recent years and so made little use of residential care for this purpose. Specialist resources elsewhere were used when required. Borough did the same but also had a resource for children with severe learning disabilities which had been unaffected by recent changes. As we shall see, this facility was managed by the disability team and was part of adult services. Managers considered that this arrangement worked well. Shortly before our fieldwork, significant developments had occurred in North in which the comparable resource, which is also part of our current research sample, had instead become managed as part of children's provision. However, it was too soon to know what the effects of this were likely to be.

Community and professional links

As we have seen, a focus of this study is the links that homes maintain with family and community and other professionals, and this was an area we explored in our interviews with managers.

During the 1980s several research studies highlighted the problems of maintaining contact between parents and children living away from home (Department of Health and Social Security 1985; Millham *et al.* 1986). This applied to both foster and residential care and most frequently involved implicit rather than explicit barriers to contact. Consequently, measures were introduced in the Children Act 1989 emphasising the importance, in most circumstances, of continuing partnership with parents. Did managers feel that these steps had made any difference? Encouragingly, this was an area in which the programme of research, its dissemination and changes in policy were thought to have paid dividends as social workers and residential staff were reported to be much more committed to maintaining family relationships. One manager referred specifically to the significantly increased budget allocated to transport for parents. The main problem perceived in this area was in Borough, where the distance separating parents and many private homes was felt to impede contact.

Relationships between children's homes and fieldworkers were felt to vary considerably. For South, the introduction of the purchaser–provider structure was said to have led to a deterioration on this front. One manager stated that: 'The purchaser–provider split reinforces the fact that the fieldworker is in the driving seat: I always thought we should be working together'. His colleague observed independently: 'This purchaser–provider split – I wouldn't recommend it to anybody. You spend all your time fighting each other and the kids get lost'. It was added that it was not always made clear exactly what tasks were being delegated to the residential home. This was made worse in cases where the fieldworker did not forward a copy of the care plan to the children's home, which was not an uncommon occurrence as we were to discover.

Our study took place when concern was growing about the educational experiences of pupils living in children's homes. Academic achievements were felt to be poor and high rates of school exclusion were reported (Brodie and Berridge

1996; Department of Health Social Services Inspectorate and Office for Standards in Education 1995). This emerged as an important theme in our research and we deal with it in greater detail later. However, at this stage, we asked managers for their views on the links between residential homes and education professionals. In response it was confirmed that this was undoubtedly an area of weakness, which had several dimensions. These spanned, for example, relationships between managers in education and social services, the educational environment of children's homes, and links between children's homes and individual schools. All this was felt to be particularly problematic in Borough, where children in private sector homes – usually outside London – would need to gain access to local education authority resources. Understandably, not all LEAs would welcome the influx of difficult children with whom London schools had been unable to cope. Increasing numbers of private homes offered education on site, which solved certain problems for social workers. However, the education department in Borough was often dissatisfied with the breadth of curriculum and quality of education provided, and therefore refused to recognise some private homes. Consequently, education sometimes refused to meet schooling costs. All this was not helped by the reported running down of educational provision for pupils with emotional and behavioural difficulties in the capital and elsewhere, a point that was also emphasised in North.

In addition, we inquired into links between children's homes and health professionals. At an individual level, the health care offered to children was not a major concern and GPs, for example, were felt to be supportive. In light of other evidence, however, perhaps we should not be quite so complacent (Brodie, Berridge and Beckett 1997). A major concern was the absence of strong *structural* links between social services and health. Some training input had been provided by health professionals, yet little consultancy was provided to staff groups and there was not a significant input to residential homes from clinical (and educational) psychologists or child psychiatrists. The exception to this, as we shall see, was in the homes catering for disabled children, where managers indicated a much more integrated approach.

Overall assessment

We ended our interviews with managers by asking them to summarise what they felt were the main achievements over recent years in their residential services and what were the current major problems. A range of structural improvements was reported, including reducing the size of homes and investing in their physical maintenance and appearance. Staffing initiatives were also highlighted, including better induction procedures, training and staff supervision and appraisal. Improved co-ordination between foster and residential care was reported in two agencies. Furthermore, perhaps with our presence in mind, reference was made to the positive benefits of dissemination of results from the major research programmes of the decade (Department of Health 1991d, 1995a).

It may be an accurate reflection of the period, or something about the nature of social workers, but managers had more to say about current problems in residential child care rather than achievements. There was much overlap in the accounts of managers in North and South. Most emphasis was placed on the way in which children's homes were currently used: there was a lack of clarity about the specific roles of some homes, too many placements continued to be made in emergencies and, as a consequence, the combination of children in individual homes was often inappropriate. Problems were perceived to persist also in the functioning of fieldworkers in relation to residential care: one manager alleged prejudice against this service, which had its roots in social work qualifying training; while, perhaps in contrast, another argued there was insufficient gatekeeping and creative use of alternatives to residence. The other main issue raised by managers in these two authorities concerned the deterioration in educational experiences of children living in residential homes, especially in relation to non-attendance and exclusion from school.

In Borough, managers reiterated several of the points discussed already in this chapter, namely that the privatisation policy overall would lead to inferior care for children and make it less likely that placements would be adequately monitored.

Conclusion

In later chapters we can observe the extent to which life in our 12 children's homes seems to have been influenced by the factors identified in our interviews with managers. It will also be interesting to discover whether there is consistency between the perceptions of managers and those of other research participants. However, the overall impression gained from interviews with managers is one of pessimism and it does not bode well for what is to follow.

Some areas of progress were clearly identified in these interviews. As we saw, managers were confident that residential homes were now more positively disposed towards children's families and better at encouraging contact. If so – and we did seek evidence – this would be an important achievement. In general, however, the picture that emerged is discouraging. Managers had much more to say about problems than achievements. There was also little to suggest that the authorities concerned had developed the positive role for residential care endorsed in official reports (Department of Health 1991a, b; Wagner 1988). Special circumstances had obviously arisen in Borough, but there were a number of common concerns in North and South.

Three main themes seem to emerge from these management interviews that are relevant to following chapters. First, it was apparent that each of our three local authorities had experienced profound changes in their children's and residential services. This is not necessarily unexpected or a bad thing. Indeed, the past decade has witnessed substantial redirection in most areas of social policy – education, health, housing, income support and so on. Within the personal social services, community care reforms have had considerable implications for adult users. Yet the recent development of child care services has been significantly different to other areas of social policy – as was argued in Chapter 1. At least up to the time of writing, many of the main ideological influences of Conservative legislation over the 1980s and '90s have been absent in child care (but see Chapter 8). Though some might disagree (Parton 1991), the Children Act seems unique among social policy legislation of the period for its incremental approach and welfare aspirations (Berridge 1995b; Packman and Jordan 1991). Radical change in services, therefore, would not necessarily have arisen due to the policy framework.

No doubt managers would point to the general financial climate as leading to changes. Supportive evidence comes from Schorr (1992), who has argued that the personal social services were severely under-funded during this period. Indeed, managers in South and Borough maintained that changes in residential provision were essentially finance-led. Thus over the past decade, there was a diminution in residential places of three-quarters in North and South, while Borough dismantled its service completely. A major development in our study areas was that the availability of larger specialist residential resources, such as CHEs or homes with observation and assessment, had been severely curtailed, if not discontinued. In our 1985 study no fewer than a third of all residents had lived previously in an O & A, usually as first placement on leaving home. This was virtually unknown for our current group and, no doubt, children's homes were fulfilling many of the emergency reception and assessment functions previously served by O & As. Hence, for adolescents, the only residential options often seemed to be children's homes or secure provision. As we pointed out, the disappearance of this intermediate tier of placements would also have major educational implications, and local schools would assume responsibility for children who, a decade previously, frequently would have attended residential schools.

The extent of change is also reflected in some stark facts emerging from our research. Sixteen of the original group of 20 homes had closed within a decade. Only 4 of the 136 staff encountered in 1985 were still residential social workers in the same agencies 10 years on. Moreover, of the three senior managers responsible for residential services who were our main links with the authorities, *none* was still employed by the agency at the time our fieldwork ended. These are not encouraging signs and it would be difficult to envisage similar upheaval affecting other social institutions such as schools or hospitals.

Linked with the above, a second main theme arising from management interviews concerned organisational structures and their effects. Though not imposed by the legislation, each of our authorities nevertheless had introduced a system of internal markets into their children's services and had adopted various forms of 'purchaser–provider' structure. Most management comments were strongly critical of these arrangements. A particular effect was said to be that it widened the existing rift between fieldworkers (care managers) and residential staff. There is a growing social policy literature about markets in social care, much of it initially concerning health care provision (Harrison and Wistow 1992; Le Grand and Bartlett 1993; Wistow et al. 1992). Several of these authors have highlighted some of the dangers and false assumptions, for example demonstrating that we actually have not pure markets in an economic sense but 'agency-led, quasi-markets'. There are also issues concerning users and the extent and nature of choice they are able to exercise.

The arrival of internal markets in child care, according to these managers, occurred as an extension of the model for adult services and the specific implications for children had often not been discussed in detail. There is so far little literature on this subject. Jones and Bilton (1994) concluded that, 'purchaser–provider separation is not an appropriate model for the organisation of children's services' (p.54). An audit of organisational structures undertaken by the National Foster Care Association also revealed that managers had strong reservations about the influence of purchaser–provider structures on the management and delivery of foster care (Waterhouse 1997). In addition, Barker (1996) has pointed to the dangers of the underlying assumptions specifically for child protection: especially the encouragement of fragmentation rather than co-ordination, profit rather than professionalism, short-termism rather than planning, and competition rather than co-operation. Of course, structures may be less important than what occurs within them (Sinclair, Garnett and Berridge 1995). Nonetheless, it is ironic that while professionals have been critical of the effects of internal markets enforced in other services, they have been introduced voluntarily to child care where they are perhaps least appropriate.

A final major theme stemming from these interviews concerns the professional and managerial isolation of children's homes. It was reported that improvements had taken place in in-service training, often linked to National Vocational Qualifications, which is felt to have had benefits. However, relationships with fieldworkers were often said to be problematic. Links with education colleagues were underdeveloped and there were few structural links with health. These factors were also evident in 1985. As we shall see, children's homes now are probably less *socially* isolated than they were, although there is still a sense of severance or disconnectedness which, oddly, is reinforced rather than alleviated by the physical location of most homes in urban areas (see Chapter 5).

External management of homes was also problematic. Those in North were reported to have received little external supervision and in South the model introduced, initially at least, had not worked well. Indeed, during our participant observation visits in South we seldom encountered group managers in the homes. External monitoring by Borough of private sector placements was acknowledged to be poor. In a period in which the significance of external management of children's homes has been emphasised in several official reports, as shown earlier, these findings would probably suggest that our homes now received less effective external management, in terms of quantity and quality, than did the 1985 equivalents. There was a trend for the most senior manager with specific responsibility for children and families to have been downgraded from second to third tier, thus diluting expertise. In addition, the posts of middle managers who acted specifically as supervisors of, and offered support to, homes no longer existed in our three authorities. These forms of management may not always have been as effective as they might and certainly did not prevent the major scandals occurring in Staffordshire, Leicestershire and elsewhere. Yet it is difficult to see how these developments in themselves are likely to lead to enhanced residential experiences for children, let alone specifically ensure their safety.

Summary points

- Over the past decade, both North and South had reduced the number of residential places by three-quarters. The latter had also closed three CHEs and two homes with O & A facilities. Many of these decisions were reported to be finance-led.

- Due also to a financial crisis, Borough had closed all of its own residential facilities apart from a home offering short-term breaks for children with severe learning disabilities. Managers were concerned about the quality of care offered to children by some private homes; their distance from London; problems in maintaining contacts with families; and the placement of black children in predominantly white areas. There were also difficulties in monitoring placements and ensuring pupils' access to schools.

- It was possible to ascertain reasons for closure of 12 of the original 16 homes. Half were reported to be because the model and/or methods of care were considered to be no longer appropriate. The others concerned, in equal numbers, voluntary homes ceasing to be used by the local authority, unsuitable premises and dissatisfaction with the quality of care provided.

- Each of the three departments was organised according to purchaser–provider structures. Managers were mainly critical of these arrangements, a point reinforced by the wider literature.

- On the whole, departments' child care policies did not express a positive role for residential child care. Not all homes were reported to have Statements of Purpose.

- Little progress had been made in the residential care of girls and children from minority ethnic groups. In Borough, overall, care for the latter was reported to have deteriorated.

- Managers did not report strong structural links between residential homes and education and health professionals.

- Encouragingly, it was stated that homes were better in maintaining links with children's families.

- Three main themes were identified from management interviews. First, the degree of change in the three authorities. Second, organisational structures and their effects, and finally the professional and managerial isolation of homes. There was evidence that external management of homes had weakened since 1985.

4

Categories of Children's Homes and their Residents

We now turn to the sample of the 12 children's homes themselves and what occurred within them. Deciding on the starting point has been difficult. It is desirable to introduce children as soon as possible into the analysis, yet their characteristics and circumstances were so diverse that this information needs to be structured in some way for it to make sense. The logical way of approaching this, we feel, is to develop categories of home and describe the groups of residents in each. This, therefore, is the present task; the following chapter, based on our participant observation data, elaborates the styles of, and daily experiences in, homes.

The identification of different categories of home among our 12 required careful thought. As explained in Chapter 1, three types of home were described in the 1985 study. These were depicted according to size and leadership style: small, traditional 'family group-style' homes; medium-style 'adolescent hostels'; and the larger 'multi-purpose' style homes. The first and third of these categories were no longer evident in our three local authorities and so a new classification would need to be developed. A contemporary study of children's homes, with a much larger sample than ours (n=48), concluded that such a typology was not possible – most homes simply described themselves as 'general' or 'multi-purpose' (Sinclair and Gibbs 1996). Indeed, grouping homes according to size, intake, function, approach and so on proved difficult for us. It was complicated by the fact that, in comparison with 1985, the organisational structure of local authority homes had become more homogeneous. They were mostly of a similar size and there was much resemblance in management and staffing arrangements. On this occasion, there was more evidence of specialism and age differentiation of children but this was certainly not universal. Thus a categorisation may perhaps work for most homes but be difficult for all.

As our fieldwork progressed, a possible classification seemed to be emerging regarding the roles that homes fulfilled in relation to children's families. There were those that provided or facilitated family support or family assessment. Other homes dealt with the consequences of family breakdown or helped arrange *new* families. There was also preparation for what is euphemistically termed 'independence' where young people would be developing their own households and soon, perhaps, families. However, this model did not hold up and soon became too complex.

Eventually, we decided on a rather more common sense yet comprehensible classification and one that tended to be used within agencies themselves. It has been possible with our sample of 12 homes but may be more difficult elsewhere. We have found these groupings useful in our analysis of the data and, as we shall see, categories of home had certain characteristics. The categories are listed in Table 4.1, together with a brief description of each of the homes at the time of our visit.

We therefore decided eventually on the four groupings of homes shown above. The first three groups of local authority homes are categorised according to client group. (There were no children with severe learning disabilities living in homes other than 'H' and 'I'.) Private homes contained more mixed populations and, as we shall see, had other characteristics that made them distinctive.

Thus it was interesting to observe that both North and South had developed facilities specifically for younger children. Borough had intended the same before its plans were abruptly changed. In 1985 it was commonly expressed by managers that younger children, say below 12 years of age, should not live in residential homes because family environments were more suitable. This was despite the evidence that breakdowns in foster placements were not infrequent, including where younger children were involved (Berridge and Cleaver 1987). Policy documents in 1985 frequently prohibited children's home placements for this group, although in effect residential care was used as suitable alternatives were not always available.

Our evidence suggests that there has been a change in policy on this issue and the three authorities acknowledged that children's homes can perform a valuable role for younger children in specific circumstances. It was interesting to note that North and South had taken the step of developing special units for this population rather than mixing them with older residents. Private homes continued to have more of an age mix, although these were sometimes sibling groups. The two homes for younger children were involved in helping to find professional foster placements for their residents, most of whom had previously experienced placement breakdowns. The majority of residents had experienced different forms of abuse, often sexual, and staff were also trying to help to deal with this.

Two of the sample of homes offered planned short-term breaks for children with severe learning disabilities and additional health needs. One of these also contained a small, longer-stay group as well as a diverse ethnic population. It was explained in Chapter 2 how these homes came to be represented in our research. Significantly, they were the only facilities in the study offering family support on

Table 4.1 Classification system used in the study

Home   Summary details

Local authority homes for adolescents

A   A home with two male and two female residents aged between 13 and
       16 years. Located on a main road in a busy urban area. Its purpose was
       described as providing short-term emergency care and to plan for return
       home or transfer to an alternative placement (North).

B   Home with four females and one male (15–18 years) on a highly deprived
       council estate. Purpose to prepare for independent living (North).

C   Facility for three females and one male aged 14–16 years located in
       residential area. Functions rather vague (North).

D   Four females and one male living in home on council estate, age range
       13–17 years. Flexible role (South).

E   Large detached house in pleasant small town catering for five young men
       and two women (12–17 years). Intention to provide therapeutic resource
       for difficult adolescents, some of whom would otherwise be in secure
       provision (South).

Local authority homes for younger children

F   Home to prepare younger children (4–12 years) for family placement
       – four boys and two girls. Situated on council estate (North).

G   Five boys and three girls, aged 8–13 years, living in home in urban area.
       Purpose same as F (South).

*Local authority homes offering short-term breaks for young people with severe learning
disabilities and additional health needs*

H   Eight children and young women 11–15 years, together with a 23-year-old,
       staying for a week in a rather institutional-looking building in a pleasant
       neighbourhood (North).

I   Home providing at the time of the visit for seven males and six females,
       6–18 years, in built-up area in London. Places include two emergencies
       and four long-stay residents (Borough).

Private children's homes

J   Six boys and two girls (8–14 years) living in very pleasant setting – large
       rambling house close to village by the south-east coast. Performs range of
       functions in what is intended to be a homely setting.

K   Large Victorian house near to south coast accommodating four boys and
       one girl aged 13–16 years. Difficult resident group, some of whom it was
       claimed would otherwise be in secure provision.

L   Terraced house in attractive street in inner London accommodating four
       males (10–16 years) at time of visit. Described as offering therapeutic
       services to young people that local authorities often cannot deal with.

a planned, regular basis. Many of these children and young people required high levels of personal physical care. Behavioural problems were also in evidence. As serious health difficulties were common and all had statements of special educational need, it was interesting to observe how the two homes managed relationships with other professionals.

Another three establishments were private children's homes, used by Borough especially but also South. There was overlap between these and certain other homes regarding intake and function. However, they were also different in important respects: this included the contractual relationship with the local authority and style of management – two, for example, were part of larger groups. In addition, two of the homes were located in rural settings some distance from the authority and had their own educational provision.

But the largest group in our sample, and also the one most difficult to categorise, was local authority homes for adolescents. Five of our 12 homes came within this group but they accommodated just over a third of all residents. When children's homes are being discussed, or when one reads and hears about them in the media, it seems to be generally assumed that they are all of this type. Indeed, they probably generate the most trouble. However, we shall reveal that there are other patterns of residence with quite different approaches. Levels of effectiveness also vary significantly. Nonetheless, the homes for adolescents had often faced considerable problems, not all of which by any means were caused by young people. They had also witnessed considerable change.

When we visited, the 12 homes accommodated a total of 77 children and young people. The five adolescent homes had excess capacity and were slightly less than three-quarters full. In contrast, the two facilities for younger children and the same number offering short-term breaks had only two vacancies in total, while the three private homes had only four unfilled spaces. On average, the 12 homes were about half the size of the 1985 sample, with just over 6 residents in each compared with the earlier 12. Given the publicised problems of the residential sector, we were perhaps surprised not to find any homes with very high vacancy levels or that were running down. Even where acute problems were being experienced, it was interesting to note that homes were still kept quite full. Places were clearly at a premium. The home with the highest vacancy rate (three unfilled places out of eight) had experienced major behavioural problems the previous year, including a death in a road traffic accident of a male youth who had stolen a car and a recent joint suicide attempt by three female residents.

The following chapter gives more detail about the 12 homes in operation. However, having broadly introduced the different sectors, let us first see who lived there.

Residents in children's homes

Jackie is 15 and has been living in a children's home in South for only ten days. She was placed there on an emergency basis following the breakdown in her placement in another children's home in the same city. In fact, Jackie's care experience has been characterised by disruption and changes in placement – this is her fourth children's home. She was first looked after at the age of 13 when school staff expressed concern that she was 'at risk' of involvement in prostitution. Since then allegations of sexual abuse have also come to light. Jackie can be volatile and her habit of cutting her arms has aroused considerable concern. Residential staff feel ill-equipped to deal with this but so far no external support has been sought. Although Jackie is considered to be academically bright, she is an irregular attender at school and only the efforts of her head of year have so far prevented an exclusion.

Shaun's family has been known to social services for several years and his older stepsister is accommodated in another children's home. Shaun's name was placed on the child protection register at the age of five, when it was discovered that he had been physically abused by his father, who has a reputation for violent behaviour. During the next two years, the relationship between Shaun's mother and father steadily deteriorated and Shaun experienced two short-term foster placements. The second of these broke down when a foster carer had to go into hospital. This led to Shaun's placement in South's home for younger children. He has now been living there for eight months and residential staff are increasingly anxious that another foster placement should be found for him. Over recent weeks his behaviour has deteriorated and his keyworker believes that this is largely due to the delay in finding such a placement. Shaun himself desperately wants to go home but professionals agree this is unlikely to happen.

Anita is an extrovert ten-year-old. She has had a severe learning disability since birth, has minimal hearing and suffers from epilepsy. At times her behaviour can be very difficult to control, especially when she is being washed or bathed. Anita has taken part in short-term breaks for most of her life and is well known to staff at the home. She enjoys the time she spends there and interacts well with the other children. Her mother, who is divorced, has a part-time job but few social networks from which to find support. Over the past year she has also spent several weeks in hospital. This has led to an increase in the amount of short-term care Anita receives. The staff at the home are now trying to arrange for some home support in the evenings.

Residential staff describe Derek as a 'very angry young man'. He is 15 years old and has been looked after in a private children's home in the south-east for five months. This is his second placement. The first, in the London borough from which Derek originates, proved unsuccessful due to his offending behaviour. He has a lengthening criminal record, which involves a string of petty crimes. He also talks about his involvement with drugs and claims that his ambition is to be a drug dealer. Derek's educational history is confusing and most of the relevant information appears to have been lost along the way. However, it has clearly included a series of school failures. His family background is equally troubled: his mother is an alcoholic and he has a poor relationship with his stepfather. The purpose of his placement at his current home is to enable Derek to sever contact with his delinquent social network. The success of this strategy is doubtful as Derek has already made some new contacts in the locality of the home. However, the fact that the home provides on-site education does mean that Derek receives some schooling. Residential staff feel that the long-term prognosis is nevertheless poor. They are also frustrated at the lack of social work input into his case and complain that this has served to exacerbate Derek's already considerable problems.

The above brief sketches are examples of residents living in the four types of home. They are obviously not intended to be representative of the wider groups, but we have selected illustrations that would share a number of characteristics with peers. (As elsewhere in this report, certain details have been altered to preserve anonymity.) The 77 residents as a group clearly posed considerable problems for staff charged with their welfare, which cold statistics cannot fully represent. Nonetheless let us look more closely at the overall profile. This will be followed by a comparison with the 1985 population.

Biographical information about residents was gathered on pre-designed schedules. Sometimes we did this ourselves from case records but, as explained in Chapter 2, more usually it was done in association with a senior member of staff or keyworker. This process yielded an interesting insight, namely that staff were often very poorly informed about children's backgrounds and circumstances. This applied particularly in homes for adolescents and two of the private homes, whereas staff working with younger children and those who were disabled were much better informed. Thus staff in the former categories often would not know whether or not a young person's name was listed on a child protection register. Outside London they tended to be unaware of the exact ethnic backgrounds of children from minority groups: 'Well she's black isn't she?' insisted one head of home. This is despite the requirements of the Children Act 1989 Section 22(5)(c) to take into account children's religious persuasion, racial origin and cultural and linguistic background. Similarly, staff frequently looked at us bemused when we inquired if children had statements of special educational need.

This seems very unsatisfactory. It was obviously complicated by the fact that some residents had arrived only recently. It had not been helped in some cases where social workers had forwarded little information to the residential unit. Some heads of homes commented that, in purchaser–provider structures, there can be a tendency to be given only that information that is relevant to the specific tasks that are being delegated. Case files in homes were noticeably less detailed than in 1985, when bulging filing cabinets were common. Yet an equally significant reason for staff unawareness was that existing information often had not been read or its contents memorised. The *Looking After Children* initiative should be helpful in this respect, which contains good documentation for summarising key information (Department of Health 1995d). There has previously been a misguided tendency in sections of residential care for staff not to read children's records so as not to 'pre-judge' them. There was not strong evidence of this in the current study and it was not so much that staff were actively discouraged from reading files, more that their significance was often unappreciated. The notable exception to this was in a private home, where the proprietor discouraged staff from reading case records. The file of one child highlighted that he had previously mutilated animals, a point that the proprietor curiously said he had deliberately *not* communicated to the keyworker.

Individual characteristics

As shown in Figure 4.1, and was also the situation in 1985, there were slightly more males than females living in the 12 homes. However, this masks differences between the sectors and girls were in a majority in the adolescent homes: there are interesting gender issues here that have been little explored. The same gender balance applied to the two short breaks homes, which was influenced by the fact that the home in North at the time of our visit was accommodating an all-female group. (Usually, however, males seem to outnumber females in short-term care for disabled children (Office of Population Censuses and Surveys 1989).) Although it was not always possible, these eight adolescents attended regularly as a group one week in every six. They had been doing this for two years and knew each other well. There was also the advantage that they were fellow pupils at school. Thus, for most, it seemed to be considered an enjoyable social occasion and the stresses associated with moving to an unfamiliar environment and with a group of peers were minimised. We are not suggesting that short-term breaks for disabled children are always arranged this effectively (Robinson 1996a, b). Nonetheless, we did not find the three other categories of home using their facilities in such a planned way to provide family support, which will become an important recurring theme throughout this study.

Overall, the average (median) age of our sample of children was 13 years (Table 4.2). For the four categories it was, respectively, adolescents – 15 years, younger children – 10 years, short breaks homes – 13 years and private homes also 13 years. The youngest resident was a delightful four-year-old in North. She had been looked after since she was two and, through no fault of her own, had experienced no fewer than two breakdowns in planned long-term foster placements, another temporary fostering and the current residential placement. Within a year, therefore, she had experienced four placements. Staff were convinced that the next foster placement must not fail, but the consequence was that she had been living at the residential home for 18 months while a suitable family was awaited. While in the children's home, the girl was allocated members

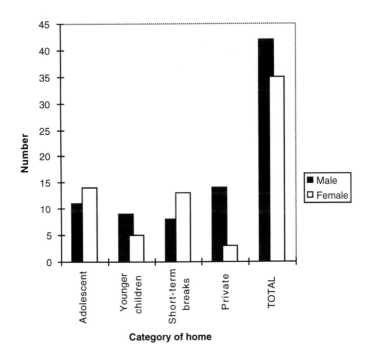

Figure 4.1 Gender of residents by category of home

of staff to work with her individually. All involved appreciated that this was unsatisfactory but it was felt preferable to repeated failures in what were intended to be permanent alternative arrangements. (An appropriate family was subsequently found and, at the time of writing, she had been living there a year and all was going to plan.)

It is generally felt that the population of children's homes is becoming older over time. This had certainly occurred in the 20 years preceding the 1985 study (Berridge 1985, Chapter 3). In 1991 the Utting Report stated that this trend was continuing. However, our evidence would not suggest that this has occurred in our three authorities over the past ten years. There is obviously the introduction of the short-term breaks category, which spans age groups and should encourage us to re-conceptualise residential care in future. Even if this group is omitted so as to be consistent with 1985, the age structure of our sample is still broadly similar to before. If anything, there are slightly more pre-adolescents and fewer over-16s. It will be important to bear in mind that our sample, overall, is somewhat younger than that portrayed in the national statistics (Department of Health 1996a) and the York research (Sinclair and Gibbs 1996). However, we emphasise the point that, although national child care trends may move in a particular direction, within this there will be much variation between individual local authorities (R. Parker, personal communication). This was also demonstrated in Rowe *et al.'s* (1989) detailed study of child care outcomes in six local authorities, which revealed strong contrasts in patterns of care and the age structure of admissions.

Table 4.2 Ages of children by category of home

Category	Age (years)				
	Under 5	6–11	12–15	16+	All
Adolescent	–	–	17	8	25
Younger children	1	10	3	–	14
Short-term breaks	–	9	8	4	21
Private	–	7	9	1	17
TOTAL	1	26	37	13	77
	(1%)	(34%)	(48%)	(17%)	(100%)

We can see from Table 4.2 that, in total, a third of children living in our sample of homes at the time of our visits were under 12 years of age. Consequently, we should not allow debates about residential care to be dominated exclusively by the needs of older adolescents.

A further point concerns age mix. As their name implies, adolescent and younger children's homes managed by local authorities were differentiated according to age. However, this was less evident in short breaks homes and the private sector. The York study, referred to above, highlighted the dangers of intimidation and exploitation in residential care and recommended accommodating older children separately from their younger peers. Given the particular vulnerability to abuse of disabled children (Kennedy 1996; Westcott and Cross 1996), this raises questions for the short breaks homes as well as, more generally, the private sector.

In total, 12 (16 per cent) children were from minority ethnic groups. With only one exception, these were all from Borough and therefore were living in the short breaks (4) and private sector (7) homes. The majority were African-Caribbean, reflecting the profile of the locality. The short break home (I) and one private facility (L) had staff from diverse ethnic backgrounds. However three African-Caribbean children were living in private homes outside London with only white staff. The head of home of one of these facilities did not know the ethnic background of two of these children. Concerns have been raised about the placement of London children from minority ethnic groups with independent fostering agencies long distances from the capital, and similar issues exist in relation to the private residential sector (Department of Health Social Services Inspectorate 1995a).

Disconcertingly, in more than one in four cases (29 per cent) staff were unaware of children's religious backgrounds and records did not contain the relevant information. The private homes took their responsibilities more seriously in this regard and were noticeably better informed. It may also have been less of an issue for the short breaks homes, where children lived for brief periods and communication with parents generally tended to be good in any case. Overall, 10 per cent of children and their families were said to have no practising religion, 40 per cent were described as Church of England/Protestant, 18 per cent Roman Catholic and one child was Muslim.

An important function of children's homes has long been recognised as catering for siblings, particularly as finding foster homes for (large) groups has often been problematic. This was acknowledged by the Utting Report (Department of Health 1991a). In the 1985 research two in every five children were living with a brother or sister in the same children's home. The situation is obviously different for the disabled group, who are away from home only a matter of days and where providing a break for, and from, parents and siblings is part of the package (Ames Reed 1993). The case comes to mind of a mother, clearly under considerable stress, visiting informally the home with her disabled daughter as a preliminary to regular placements. She was accompanied by her younger non-disabled son, whose disruptive and attention-seeking behaviour caused greater problems for staff (and the researcher) than most residents.

As with the original study, some siblings were found in homes for younger children (4 of the 19 residents) and private homes (5 out of 17). However, there were *no* brothers and sisters together occupying any of the 25 places in the adolescent homes. This signifies an important change over the decade and was also remarked upon in the York study (Sinclair and Gibbs 1996). Though age segregation can have other benefits, and may help minimise institutional abuse by peers, a consequence is that the ability of children's homes to keep sibling groups together is significantly reduced. Authorities may instead be turning to the private sector for this purpose, which, as we have seen in our small sample, is more flexible in its admissions. The Utting Report, referred to above, identified an important specific function for children's homes as catering for sibling groups, yet it appears that this contribution is diminishing. It would be useful for research to investigate what now happens to sibling groups when family breakdown occurs and as children move through the care system.

Legal status

The legal status of residents is shown in Table 4.3, where some interesting differences emerge between sectors. As one would anticipate, most disabled residents were accommodated according to a series of placements, with the exception of the small longer-stay group in Borough (I). A higher proportion than we would have expected, some three-quarters in adolescent homes, were being looked after as a result of a voluntary agreement with parents. In contrast, the same proportion of residents in younger children's homes was subject to court orders and their separation from families was more formalised. Private homes contained a mixture of the two, reflecting the diverse circumstances in which they were used. We encountered no instances of emergency protection orders and, interestingly, there were only two remands to care. Early on in our fieldwork in South there was much discussion about this latter category and the problems it caused. This included specific conditions imposed by courts, such as curfews or restriction to buildings, which were difficult for staff to enforce. Though we did not gather retrospective information, we were informed that remands to the residential sector had increased but, following problems in controlling several of the young people concerned and guaranteeing their appearance at court, the local authority successfully encouraged magistrates to pursue alternative strategies (see also Berridge et al. 1995). The 'other' category in Table 4.3 also includes three interim care orders.

Table 4.3 Legal status by category of home

Category	Voluntary agreement	Series	Care orders	Emerg. protect.	Other	All
Adolescent	19	–	3	–	3	25
Younger children	3	–	9	–	2	14
Short-term breaks	3	17	1	–	–	21
Private	7	–	8	–	2	17
TOTAL	32	17	21	–	7	77
	(42%)	(22%)	(27%)	(0%)	(9%)	(100%)

Comparisons with the situation in 1985 are difficult due to changes in the legislation. Nonetheless, even if one excludes the short break group, broadly equal numbers of children are now being accommodated voluntarily as are subject to court orders. In the earlier study, local authorities had complete legal control in three-quarters of cases. This suggests that social services departments are working more often in partnership with parents as the Children Act 1989 intended.

An important related legal issue concerns children whose names are entered on child protection registers, indicating that their safety requires an inter-agency plan. Although in the past too many general cases of 'children in need' may have been unnecessarily caught up in the child protection system (Department of Health and Social Security 1995; Gibbons, Conroy and Bell 1995), registration is a serious issue that imposes important responsibilities on carers. As shown in Table 4.4, one in six residents were currently in need of special protection measures and for the same number this had applied at some stage in the past. Child abuse concerns were very significant for the younger children category (4 out of 14 currently on registers, the same number as previously) and had also been an important feature for the private homes' population (3 from 17 now, 7 earlier). However, we should not assume that it is only young children who are at risk, and one in five residents in adolescent homes were also currently named on child protection registers. Full information was not available on all these cases, but three of the five were boys and concerns ranged across physical, sexual and emotional abuse and neglect. They were aged from 12–15 years.

As stated earlier, it was disconcerting to learn that staff were unaware that eight residents, one in ten of the total, were named on registers. Four of these were in short breaks homes but there were also two each in adolescent and private facilities. While it might be suggested that if there were major child protection concerns the homes would have known about them, it would be dangerous and misconceived to make this assumption. There is also not the excuse that all had recently arrived as, of the latter groups, one had been resident for six months and the other nearly a year. Lack of information about disabled children's backgrounds has been highlighted by other research (Stalker and Robinson 1991).

Table 4.4 Child protection registration by category of home

Category	Registration status				
	Currently on child protection register	Previously on child protection register	Never on child protection register	Information missing	All
Adolescent	5	1	17	2	25
Younger children	4	4	6	–	14
Short-term breaks	1	1	15	4	21
Private	3	7	5	2	17
TOTAL	13	13	43	8	77
	(17%)	(17%)	(56%)	(10%)	(100%)

Special needs

Most residents in the 12 homes had been assessed as having special needs or a disability (Table 4.5). This is obviously influenced by the inclusion in our sample of the two establishments for children with severe learning disabilities, the majority of whom also had physical disabilities. Their conditions included cerebral palsy, autism, spinal injury, epilepsy and hyperactivity. Some children had no speech and no hearing. Staff had to give one girl enemas on each occasion for her to use the toilet. There were also rare medical problems such as non-ketotic hyperglycinemia, fragile X syndrome and chromosomal abnormality. Some children had limited life expectancy and one severely disabled boy, who had been steadily losing weight, subsequently died.

Table 4.5 Special needs and disabilities of residents by category of home

Category	Special needs/disability							
	Physical sensory disability	Chronic health problem	Moderate learning difficulty	Severe learning disability	Emotional behaviour difficulty	More	None	All
Adolescent	3	2	–	–	2	–	18	25
Younger children	2	–	2	–	4	–	6	14
Short-term breaks	–	–	3	4	–	12	–	21
Private	2	1	3	–	2	2	7	17
TOTAL	7	3	8	4	8	14	31	77
	(9%)	(4%)	(11%)	(5%)	(11%)	(19%)	(41%)	(100%)

There were ten more children assessed as having a physical/sensory disability or serious health problem living in the other three categories of home: these included hearing and visual impairments, epilepsy and asthma. They also contained another 13 residents whom educational psychologists had assessed as having moderate learning difficulties or emotional and behavioural difficulties. Parker, Loughran and Gordon (1992) have pointed out that social services departments are looking after significant numbers of disabled children, many of them in non-specialist units, and this would be confirmed from our data.

Child abuse

We investigated in greater detail the reasons for children being looked after by the local authority. The short-term breaks group is omitted from what follows as the stresses associated with caring for someone with severe learning and physical impairments were identified as the specific overriding factors. Returning to issues of abuse, it was asked to what extent this was an area of concern. Figure 4.2 reveals that abuse in its various forms had been a common experience in the lives of the

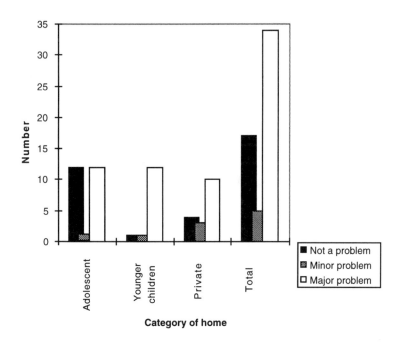

Figure 4.2 Extent to which abuse is a reason for being looked after by category of home

children in the three other categories of home. Overall, in the opinion of staff and according to case records, it had been a major problem for three in every five residents and a minor problem for a further 9 per cent. Dealing with the aftermath of abuse was a main preoccupation for the 2 homes for younger children – this was a major problem for all but two of the 14 residents. Abuse had also been a key issue for the private homes' population and was significant for half the residents of the adolescent homes.

Children react differently to abuse for reasons that we do not understand. Its impact will be influenced by the form of abuse, its severity and endurance, the perpetrator(s) and context within which it occurs. A family environment that is 'low on warmth and high on criticism' (Department of Health 1995a, p.19) has been singled out as particularly damaging. Social workers and residential staff attributed a range of behaviours of children to the experience of physical, sexual and emotional abuse and neglect. This included aggressive outbursts, sexualised behaviour, total withdrawal, mistrust of adults, insecurity, self-injury and depression. One girl gradually lost control of her behaviour each evening as bedtime approached, requiring restraint. She injured herself with glass and knives if staff were not vigilant. Another young boy encouraged his peers to engage in sexual behaviour and masturbated as he watched. Countless children had very low self-esteem and were resigned to whatever life offered them. Clearly, many needed very special help.

Comparing these results with the situation in 1985 is again complex as identifying and responding to abuse are essentially social processes rather than objective reactions to a fixed event (Little and Gibbons 1993). One might have expected there to have been more evidence of abuse on this occasion than previously: sexual abuse of children is now more widely acknowledged and there has been a tendency for abuse issues increasingly to overshadow other child welfare concerns (Department of Health 1995a). Attempts at consistency were made by asking similar questions to the previous study and there was the advantage of one researcher's involvement in both. The result was that, on this occasion, abuse or neglect were identified as major contributory factors to being looked after in 61 per cent of cases compared with 44 per cent in the early 1980s. Though it is beyond this study to isolate the sociological processes involved in assessment, classification and depiction which underlie these responses, nonetheless abuse was acknowledged as a more significant issue in the lives of this resident group than previously.

Stress factors

The relative presence of different types of abuse was revealed when we examined the main 'stress factor' felt to be responsible for the child being looked after. This was not always easy to undertake as multiple factors are generally involved. Nonetheless, results are shown in Figure 4.3. This indicates three main groups of reasons leading to accommodation. The predominant consideration was the behavioural problems caused by the young person: general control problems at home (16), together with difficulties caused at school (2) and in the community, including offending (2). Equal concern was expressed about abuse to the child: sexual (8), physical (5), neglect (6) and sexual abuse of a parent towards another child (1). The third, more general, category concerned inadequate care (7) and relationship problems between parents and children (6). The former two categories were age-related to a certain extent, applying disproportionately to adolescent and younger children's homes, respectively. The private homes dealt with the range of problems. We reiterate that these figures exclude the short-term breaks category, where the reasons for providing accommodation were felt to be more specific.

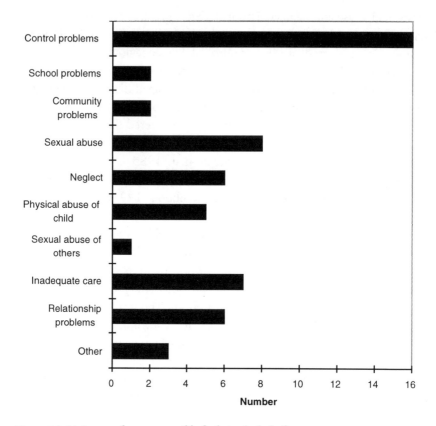

Figure 4.3 Main stress factor responsible for being looked after

We approached the same issue slightly differently in order to explore the combination of factors involved. This consisted of presenting a list of a range of over 30 factors and asking the extent to which each was felt to have contributed to leading to accommodation. These covered issues such as carers' personal problems, relationships and abuse, and contextual elements such as poverty and accommodation. The main factors are shown in Figure 4.4, which demonstrates the multiple difficulties of most children for whom a combination of serious factors usually applied. For each stress factor listed, the proportion for whom this was felt to be a 'major' problem was as follows: relationship problems at home – 82 per cent; behavioural problems of child – 66 per cent; abuse or neglect (as discussed earlier) – 61 per cent; educational problems – 59 per cent; emotional/personal problems – 50 per cent; poverty or accommodation problems – 21 per cent.

For different types of home the most significant 'major' factors were:

- adolescent homes (*n*=25) – relationship problems (23); behaviour (20); education (16)

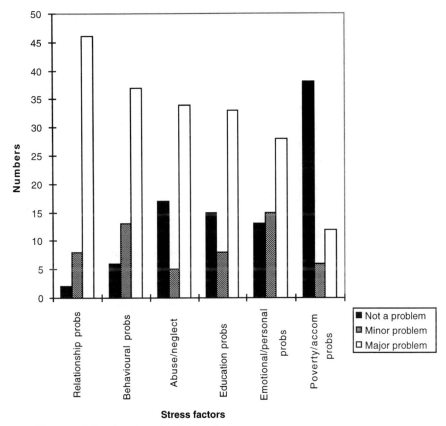

Note: Figure excludes short-term breaks population.
Figure 4.4 Significance of stress factors on decision to accommodate

- homes for younger children (n=14) – abuse (12); relationships (10); emotional/personal problems (5)
- private homes (n=17) – relationships (13); behaviour (13); education (12).

The complexity of children's lives, and the problems that are likely to confront carers, can be indicated by totalling the number of 'major' stress factors recorded for each child. Of a possible total of six, the average (median) for the three categories of home discussed here was 3.8. For the different sectors it was: adolescent homes – 3.8; younger children – 3.5; and private homes – 4.2. Approached in this way, it is clear that these homes are catering for a highly problematic group who have suffered and display a range of problems. Interestingly, the backgrounds of younger children appear only very slightly less problematic than those of adolescents. Furthermore, the most 'difficult' cases, if one can use that term, are to be found in the private homes in our sample. This is confirmed if we examine children with the highest individual scores: there were two residents in the younger children category who totalled a maximum of 6 (there were none in adolescent homes); while in the private sector one scored 6 and five residents each totalled 5.

This experience of multiple problems has important consequences. Caprara and Rutter (1995) have shown that single stressful experiences tend, on the whole, to carry low psychosocial risks, whereas: 'Serious risks tend to derive from a *combination* of adversities or stresses occurring at the same time, from meaningful *links* between a current stress and a previous adversity, or from *accumulations* of stresses/adversities over time' (p.42; authors' emphases). There is also the important point that an additional stress factor can have an overall impact that is greater than its effect in isolation (Caprara and Rutter 1995). Consistent with this, research by Pilling (1990) has demonstrated that the more socially disadvantaged children become, the more difficult and unlikely it is for them to be socially mobile and thereby 'escape' as they grow older. We did not investigate the age at which adversities commenced, which is known to be a significant factor.

On this occasion we analysed the reasons for children being looked after rather differently than in 1985. However, in some areas direct comparisons are possible. For example, restricting ourselves to major stress factors (and, again, excluding the short breaks group) 34 of the 56 (61 per cent) had been abused or neglected compared with 44 per cent in 1985; 37 (66 per cent) had caused behavioural problems at home rather than 32 per cent; and those causing problems at school had risen considerably to 33 (59 per cent) from barely a quarter. The incidence of behavioural problems prior to entry, therefore, is reported to have more than doubled.

As before, we must be cautious as social work intervention, entry to local authority accommodation and the writing of case records are very much subjective activities and social processes rather than objective responses to definite events. What we are monitoring, therefore, is as much professional activity as the circumstances of children in need and their families. Other research has demonstrated the considerable discretion exercised by professionals (Packman, Randall and Jacques 1986). With this in mind, it was nevertheless clear to us during the current study from reading detailed files and interviews with a range of participants, that children's homes are now dealing with a much more complex and problematic group of residents than before. As Gooch (1996) has put it, the 'exodus of the marginal' (p.23) has occurred. For example, an older female resident had recently served six months in prison for assault. A youth had threatened a mother and her baby with a knife. One resident poured deliberately a cup of tea over the researcher's head, although this was almost a gesture of affection as he had set alight someone's hair the week before. The mental health problems of young people in care have received little research attention. One recent report argued that two-thirds of all children accommodated in one local authority showed evidence of psychiatric disorder. A quarter were said to have a major depressive illness (*Community Care* 1996; see also McCann and Jones 1996). Furthermore, we recall the remarkable finding from the York research, where four in ten of their sample said they had considered killing themselves in the previous month (Sinclair and Gibbs 1996).

Parents

Studies of children looked after by local authorities have shown the extensive restructuring that has affected their families (Millham *et al.* 1986). This applied also to our sample (Table 4.6).

Table 4.6 Adult carers in 'home base' by category of home

Category	Carers in home base					
	Birth mother and father	Mother only	Mother-cohabiting/ stepfather	Father only	Other	All
Adolescent	7	3	11	1	3	25
Younger children	6	3	3	1	1	14
Short-term breaks	13	3	1	3	1	21
Private	2	9	2	1	3	17
TOTAL	28	18	17	6	8	77
	(36%)	(23%)	(22%)	(8%)	(10%)	(100%)

Totals may not equal 100 per cent due to rounding.

This reveals interesting differences between sectors. The majority of families for the short breaks group were still intact and residential care was providing family support. There were also three cases where fathers were helped to cope alone by providing these interludes. In the other groups, however, family structures were more varied and birth parents lived together in only a quarter of cases. Nearly a third of families were headed by lone carers. Though numbers are small, the high level of family breakdown for the private homes group is particularly striking. It is also interesting to observe that, in a third of cases, the 'home base' of residents of adolescent homes included a new male partner – actually the most common arrangement. Interestingly, bearing in mind that most residents in our adolescent homes were female, there is some evidence that girls are more likely to experience the divorce of parents than are boys. This is compounded by the fact that separation and divorce may have a more negative effect on girls than boys: girls are reported to have more difficulties in adapting to stepfamilies and adolescent girls have more conflicts with stepfathers than do their male peers (Fombonne 1996).

Managers, when interviewed, it may be recalled, stated that an area of improvement in practice over the past decade has concerned residential staff attitudes towards, and relationships with, parents. So how much contact did our sample have with a parent (see Figure 4.5)? All but one of the short breaks group were living permanently with one or both parents and so they are omitted from Figure 4.5; however we have included the four long-stay residents in the home in Borough for children with severe learning disabilities. Three of these were African-Caribbean boys and there was one Chinese girl, with ages ranging from 9 to 13 years. They were looked after in separate accommodation by their own staff. Two of the four had no parental contact. Of the other residents of the ten homes, half were in regular contact with a parent on a weekly basis and another quarter saw them monthly. Fewer than one in ten had no contact whatsoever. Managers' comments are confirmed and levels of family contact are indeed higher than in 1985. Then, equivalent figures were 41 per cent, 16 per cent and 20 per cent.

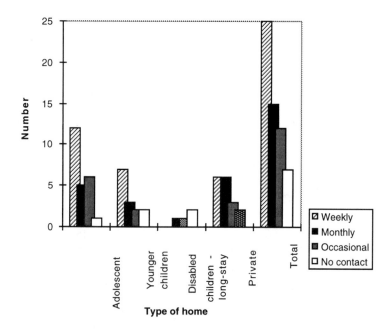

Note: Excludes the disabled group apart from four long-stay residents.
Figure 4.5 Parental contact by category of home

A further interesting point emerges from Figure 4.5. First, levels of contact were quite high in the two homes for younger children, despite the fact that the main task for the homes was to find permanent alternative family placements. It was planned in most cases that parental contact would continue after placement and this was clearly important to many of the children concerned. For example, the four-year-old mentioned earlier saw her mother regularly although there were no plans for her to return to live with her. Compared with some of the earlier, more simplistic notions of permanence – as either constituting a return home or adoption – this suggests that the concept of *permanent, open* foster care is gaining acceptance (Aldgate, Maluccio and Reeves 1989; Triseliotis, Sellick and Short 1995). More generally, this signals adherence to the defence of the birth family and parents' rights perspective rather than the 'state paternalism' approach (Fox Harding 1991). It is also consistent with the partnership philosophy advocated by the authors of 1980s child care research studies (Department of Health 1991d; Department of Health and Social Security 1985) and endorsed by the Children Act 1989.

Care careers

One might expect that the quality of the parental relationship would be influenced by how recently separation occurred. For almost half the residents of the adolescent homes, the current 'looked after' episode had lasted less than a year. The longest was eight years, with an average (median) of 1.8. Residents in the younger children category had been separated from home for longer, with an average of 3.5 years. Only 1 of the 14, in contrast, had been away from home for less than a year. The private group came somewhere in between, with an average separation of 2.7 years; while for the small, long-stay group of disabled children it was 3.3 years. However, the longest duration in public care was 15 years for a young man in a private home (see below). In the 1985 study the average total length of time in care of the sample was just over four years whereas here it is nearer 2.5. The very long stay care group, therefore, now seems to be largely absent from these children's homes. For example, in the original study two-fifths had been in public care for at least half of their lives, including a fifth who had been looked after virtually since birth. These groups are no longer evident in the current sample.

This trend is also reflected in the length of stay at the residential home itself. Almost half had been resident under six months, including three in ten less than three months. The overall average for the sample was ten months in the current home, compared with nearer two years in 1985. Adolescent homes were particularly transitory, with three-fifths of residents having been present less than three months. The average stay in private homes is affected by one facility in which six of the eight residents had been present over three years.

Despite having been in public care for an average of less than 2.5 years, many of our sample had nonetheless 'done the rounds' and in that time had experienced on average (median) 2.4 placements each. One in seven had witnessed seven or more. The record was held by a 16-year-old young man at a private home, looked after since he was very young, who in that time had experienced at least 13 placements. This included six breakdowns in foster placements, two of which were intended to be long-term, an adoption breakdown and six residential placements that had eventually collapsed. This youngster was highly problematic, with a string of offences and complex health problems. He was prescribed medication by a GP in an attempt to control his behaviour. This was carefully monitored by staff. However, the drugs had potentially dangerous side effects and the young person's safety was dependent on high levels of supervision, which could not always be guaranteed. Nonetheless, staff were making a significant effort with a difficult young man.

With the exception of this resident, the private sector group had noticeably more stable care careers than with the adolescent and younger children categories. Given that many adolescents had been in public care for relatively brief periods, it is disconcerting that the average number of placements for this group was 3.3. A third had lived in five or more different settings. As revealed in the wider research literature, this instability seems to be an integral part of the adolescent care process (Sinclair *et al.* 1995; Triseliotis *et al.* 1995).

Half of all residents had previously experienced a residential placement, rising to almost three-quarters of the adolescent homes' population (Table 4.7). Fewer had witnessed a planned long-term foster placement (27%), although other types of fostering were more common (53%), including short-term and bridging arrangements (Triseliotis, Sellick and Short 1995). Three unfortunate children who had been adopted (two living in private homes) had witnessed the breakdown of their second family as well as their first.

In total, three-fifths of these 60 children had experienced breakdowns in placements of some sort. This affected all but four of those living in homes for younger children. A quarter of the 60 had lived through residential breakdowns

Table 4.7 Number of residents experiencing previous placements by category of home

Category	Placement				
	Residential	Long-term foster	Other foster	Adoption	All
Adolescent	18	5	14	1	25
Younger children	2	7	12	0	14
Disability – long-stay	4	0	0	0	4
Private	5	4	6	2	17
TOTAL	29	16	32	3	60

Note: Excludes the disabled group apart from four long-stay residents.

Table 4.8 Number of residents experiencing previous placement breakdowns by category of home

Category	Placement				
	Residential	Long-term foster	Other foster	Adoption	All
Adolescent	8	4	11	1	25
Younger children	2	6	5	0	14
Disability – long-stay	1	0	0	0	4
Private	4	3	5	2	17
TOTAL	15	13	21	3	60

Note: Excludes the disabled group apart from four long-stay residents.

and one in five had experienced failed long-term fosterings (Table 4.8). In addition, over a third of children had suffered breakdowns in other types of fosterings – approaching half of the adolescent category. For the latter group, this had often immediately preceded entry to the children's home and is a situation that would merit closer investigation.

Once again these results are different in certain respects from the 1985 research. The current group had spent less time in public care than their predecessors and had experienced fewer moves. In the original study, remarkably, two in every five residents had lived in two or more other children's homes, the current placement being their third; now the comparative figure is halved. Furthermore, a third of the 1985 group had experienced one or more breakdowns in planned long-term foster placements; current findings put this lower at about a fifth. Moreover, on this occasion, most children in these circumstances were to be found living in homes for younger children, which functioned specifically to deal with this task. However, an important difference on this occasion is that there is evidence of the more strategic use of foster care of different types – as stated above, short-term, bridging and so on. Unfortunately, this clearly had mixed success for our population and a number had unsatisfactory experiences. As with the original study, therefore, an important contribution of residence seems to be to complement foster care, either where short- or long-term placements have failed or where they are unavailable.

Education

Returning now to our total group, we saw earlier that a majority had been defined as having special needs. This had been recognised by educational psychologists and 53 per cent had statements of special educational needs (these were pending for another 4 per cent). This applied to all those in the short-term breaks group and one in four living in adolescent homes. Interestingly, the majority in younger children's homes also had statements, as did almost half of those in private homes. Omitting disabled children, our overall figure of 35 per cent of residents with statements of special educational needs is high compared with other investigations. Comparative data are scarce. However, the Department of Health Social Services Inspectorate and OFSTED (1995) survey of children looked after by local authorities discovered a fifth with statements. Research into social work with teenagers found a lower figure of 12 per cent (Triseliotis *et al.* 1995). This reflects the severity of problems of our children's homes sample.

The current, or most recent, school attended by residents is shown in Figure 4.6. This omits four residents over school leaving age. The most common setting attended was mainstream day school. Despite the greater efforts to integrate pupils with special needs into mainstream settings, this applied to none of our short breaks category, three-quarters of whom attended day special schools for pupils with severe learning disabilities. No doubt the extent of their impairments and complex health needs would have posed significant problems for general

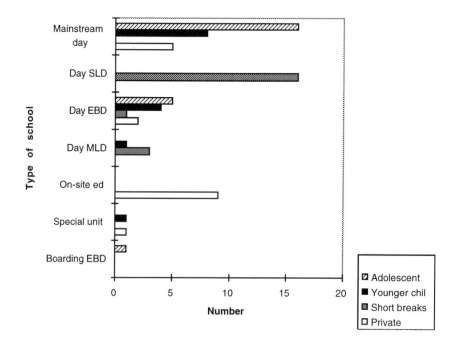

Figure 4.6 Most recent school attended by category of home

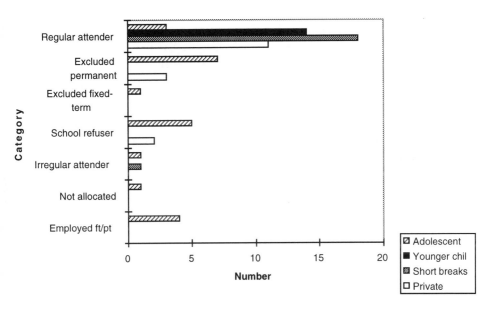

Figure 4.7 Education and employment status by category of home

settings. Day special schools for pupils with emotional and behavioural difficulties ('EBD') also played an important role for one in six residents, including a fifth of those in adolescent homes, and nearer three in ten of younger children. Significantly, more than half the pupils in private homes were educated at an on-site facility linked to the home itself, which is an important development. This pattern is in marked contrast to the 1985 findings. Then, excluding the short breaks group which was not included in the original study, 80 per cent of pupils attended mainstream schools compared with 49 per cent now; 15 per cent were at special schools in contrast to 31 per cent now; and *no* children were educated at private homes compared with 16 per cent of the current sample. It should be remembered that the age structure of the current sample is similar to that in 1985.

Although these were the schools that pupils were supposed to be attending, not all were in fact doing so (Figure 4.7). There were some marked contrasts between sectors. Most difficulties were encountered in adolescent homes and, in our preliminary visits, heads of homes and residential staff informed us that one of their greatest problems was the exclusion from school of residents who would thus be around the home all day with nothing to do. We return to this topic in the next chapter. It is also the subject of a detailed sub-study on its own (Berridge and Brodie 1996; Brodie 1995; Brodie and Berridge 1996). On close examination of case files, it was discovered that seven residents in adolescent homes were indeed permanently excluded from school and another was subject to a fixed-term exclusion of five days. Four of these had been excluded from special schools specifically for pupils with emotional and behavioural difficulties, an interesting sequence of events. The number of exclusions from special schools seems to be increasing but little research has been undertaken to date (Parsons 1996).

However, there were several other children that staff had informed us were excluded who were, in fact, not excluded but not attending for other reasons. The implications of this for the pupils concerned are serious. Five children not attending were not excluded but were school refusers. Another was an irregular attender, while a boy who had been excluded a month earlier from a residential 'EBD' school was not attending as no alternative arrangements for him had yet been made. Only three pupils in the adolescent homes out of the 21 eligible, therefore, were regularly attending school. Indeed, there were more in full- or part-time employment (four). In contrast to the current study, the problem of school exclusion did not emerge in any significant sense in the 1985 research and the phrase is not even mentioned in that report.

The issue is more complex than it may initially appear and we should hesitate before apportioning blame to social services. Most young people were exhibiting school problems prior to entry to the residential establishment, and regular non-attendance or exclusion was often a factor that hastened a deterioration in relationships and ultimate rejection from home. Therefore, it was not so much that children's homes were creating educational difficulties as dealing with their effects. But it is striking, nonetheless, that the three other sectors seemed to cope much better than adolescent homes. It is important to acknowledge that, while behavioural problems in primary schools are being reported more frequently (Hayden, Sheppard and Ward 1996), exclusions are mainly concentrated in the secondary sector (Brodie and Berridge 1996; Department for Education and Employment 1993). Most pupils in two of the private homes were being educated in on-site school facilities: there are concerns about the quality of education provided in small or satellite units (Office for Standards in Education 1995). This aspect of community homes with education was also strongly criticised in the past (Department of Education and Science 1980). Nonetheless, the vast majority of pupils were attending regularly in these two private homes. As we saw earlier, it could also be argued that the most complex and difficult cases were to be found in the private sector.

However, it was not always the older children who were necessarily the most challenging (as the next chapter will testify) and it was a notable achievement that *all* the children in the two homes for younger children were regularly attending school. Furthermore, with only one exception on serious health grounds, all school age pupils in the two short breaks homes were regular attenders at school. None were excluded. However, their behaviour was often highly problematic to teachers and residential workers. For example, one girl needed three people to wash and change her as she kicked constantly; three others were regularly violent to peers and adults; a boy tried to eat virtually everything he could lay his hands on; and another soiled and smeared furniture. Teachers even coped each day with the boy who was terminally ill. In the next chapter we consider in more detail the processes involved. However, from the evidence presented here, it would be difficult to maintain a view that exclusion from school occurs solely as a rational response to pupils' problems and the behavioural challenges they pose. We return to this theme later.

Conclusion

This chapter has contained a wide range of information about the occupants of the 12 children's homes at the time of our visits. Several themes have emerged that will be developed as the report progresses.

In the same way that we categorised residential homes, we considered whether it would be possible to identify groupings of young people. Indeed, four such categories were depicted in the 1985 study. These were, first, sets of younger siblings admitted to children's homes in emergencies for short-term shelter. Second, there was a large group of children of mixed ages (often, once again, siblings) awaiting long-term foster placements. Third were the isolated children who had spent most or all of their lives in public care and experienced repeated failures in planned long-term arrangements. Finally came the adolescents with close family links who rejected foster care.

The first of the four categories did not appear in our new sample of homes. Presumably, short-term and emergency fostering are more widely available or children in these circumstances nowadays are less likely to be looked after away from home. The second group was encountered in the two homes for younger children and in the private sector but was less relevant to the adolescent homes' population. Interestingly, we also discovered few very long-stay care cases and this begs the question of what has happened to them? Perhaps foster care arrangements are becoming more effective and those in need of long-term care eventually find a base. In recent years adoption, as a child-centred policy, has also been pursued more assertively for young people whose families offered little (Triseliotis, Shireman and Hundleby 1997, Chapter 1). Furthermore, some authorities, including North, have developed imaginative supported housing projects for older adolescents. More worrying would be the possibility that there are some rootless and drifting adolescents receiving few services and whose situation is thus precarious.

Compared with the 1985 research, this study includes an important new group of consumers of residential care: children with severe learning disabilities and their families. Not only are their characteristics distinctive but the service they received, in our sample of homes, was also unique: no others were receiving planned family support in the form of short-term breaks. We ask later why this is.

However, the major group in common with the 1985 study is the population living in what we have termed 'adolescent homes'. It is difficult to provide further differentiation but aspects of their situation have important implications. They were mostly accommodated following voluntary arrangements and, interestingly, girls were in a majority. Backgrounds of abuse and violence were not uncommon and they have experienced multiple social problems rather than difficulties in isolated areas. In the rather harsh terminology of an earlier research study, they are not 'villains' or 'victims' but display elements of both (Packman, Randall and Jacques 1986). Family relationships thus deteriorated into conflict and rejection. On entry to accommodation, schooling often had broken down or was tenuous, which posed additional stress on family members. Many arrived in residential care after a short-term fostering had failed or expired without alternative remedies. It is disconcerting to note that young people often moved frequently and rapidly between residential homes: three-quarters of our population had lived in other children's homes and no fewer than *three-fifths* had been at the current home less than three months.

The resident group overall clearly posed considerable challenges to staff in our 12 homes. We see in the next chapter how they responded.

Summary points

- Categorising the 12 homes was a complex exercise but four groupings were eventually identified: local authority (LA) homes for adolescents; LA homes for younger children; LA homes offering short breaks for young people with severe learning disabilities and additional health needs; and private children's homes. The first category was the largest.

- Compared with 1985, greater age differentiation in the local authority sector (but not private homes) was evident. The operation of homes specifically for younger children signals a policy shift at the local level.

- Though more alert to the ethical implications and their professional responsibilities concerning confidential information, staff were often poorly informed about children's backgrounds. This included, disconcertingly, essential information such as ethnic origin, religion, child protection status and whether a statement of special educational needs applied.

- Though males overall were in a majority, there were more young women than men living in adolescent and short breaks homes at the times of our visits.

- In contrast to wider evidence, in our three authorities the residential population had not aged since 1985. A third of our sample was under 12 years. Residential care still serves important functions for younger children, which should not be overlooked.

- There were far fewer siblings living together in homes than in 1985. They were present among the younger group and in private establishments but no siblings were found in the adolescent homes.

- Most children had been assessed as having special needs or a disability. A number of these were living outside the short breaks homes.

- Most residents, apart from the short breaks group, were known to have experienced serious abuse of various forms. This had increased compared with the population in 1985.

- Three main groupings of stress factors leading to accommodation were identified: behavioural problems, abuse and neglect, and, slightly less noticeably, inadequate care and relationship problems. Most children had multiple problems and had experienced severe difficulties in several aspects of their lives. Analysed in this way, the private homes' population was most 'problematic' and, interestingly, the younger children were not greatly different from the others.

- It therefore appears that the current children's homes population is much more complex and problematic than in 1985. The proportion posing behavioural problems prior to entry has more than doubled.

- Levels of family contact are higher than previously, in line with research messages and Children Act 1989 measures.

- Average length of stay at homes has more than halved compared with 1985. The adolescent group was particularly transitory, three-fifths of residents having been present under three months. Despite this, apart from the short breaks group, many children had experienced previous fostering and residential placements.

- The education of children's home residents has become a major factor and there are strong concerns about school non-attendance and exclusion. However, it was striking that, compared with the adolescent homes, the other three categories of home were much more successful in achieving attendance at school.

5

Daily Life in Children's Homes

As has already been noted, participant observation constituted the major method used in the study. Chapter 2 has outlined some of the advantages of this approach, which include the richness of descriptive accounts and the detailed insights that can emerge. There is also the opportunity to distinguish between what a children's home claims to be doing and what is actually taking place.

This chapter is, therefore, based on the participatory dimension of the study and sets out to analyse daily life in our 12 homes. It describes what homes looked like, how the daily routine was organised and the nature of interaction between young people and staff. In this way an attempt is made to capture something of the experience of living in a children's home, the humorous and the bizarre as well as the more prosaic. Whatever our study lacks in its breadth is hopefully compensated for by its depth.

It is important to recognise that, following our series of preparatory meetings, only one substantial fieldwork visit took place in each home. This inevitably influenced our results and should be borne in mind in their interpretation, especially as the timing of entry to a research setting can have an effect on the findings which emerge. While children's homes do not have a cyclical year in quite the same way as do schools, other cycles do occur in the form of the young person's stay within the home. During our visits we could not, of course, guarantee observation of such important events as departures and arrivals. We also found that the equilibrium in a children's home is typically a fragile one and changes to the internal dynamics of any home can occur. This is largely related to the transient nature of the resident population, staff shifts and absence, and unpredictability in young people and their circumstances.

Nonetheless, the observations which took place were as detailed as possible, each occupying four or five days, and our visits coincided with a range of events and situations occurring within the 12 homes. While it was rarely possible to sleep-in overnight, we stayed nearby and visited each of the homes from early morning to late evening – approximately 13 hours each day. We were therefore able to observe the day's events across shifts and participated in as many activities as possible. This involved us in everything from sewing name labels on new clothes, visits to parks and swings, and playing seemingly interminable games of

Monopoly. We made sure we were also present in some homes during weekends and school holidays as well as weekdays. However, while arguably some of the most important events in a children's home take place in the early hours of the morning, this was not usually a practical option.

All this yielded a mass of fascinating data. In order to ensure coherence and maximise the comparison with the earlier study, we had developed a structured participation observation schedule. While the guide was important in focusing observation, we also recorded a range of incidents which seemed to be significant in understanding the life of the home. Our sociological approach entailed recording information throughout the day rather than during specific, measured, time-limited intervals (McCall and Simmons 1969).

This chapter follows the outline of the observation schedule, moving from the physical appearance of the children's homes to an examination of the pattern of daily life within the units, the nature of interaction between young people and staff, and the type of activity in which the two groups were involved. The nature of the links between the children's home and young people's families, schools and the surrounding community will also be considered. However, we start with the purpose of homes.

Aims and objectives

Providing written evidence of the aims and objectives of children's homes is a legal requirement and, in view of this, we expected little difficulty in obtaining the necessary information. The guidance on residential care which accompanies the Children Act 1989 makes clear that each children's home should have a Statement of Purpose and Function (Department of Health 1991b). In making this requirement the guidance acknowledges the increased specialisation of children's homes, and notes that the provision of Statements of Purpose should aid those with responsibility for making placement decisions and in the development of good practice. The Statement of Purpose should include a range of information, including some indication of the ethos or guiding principles of the home, a description of what the home does and the manner in which care is provided. Aims and objectives should be, 'as concrete as possible, clearly attainable and capable of being measured' (p.5). Statements, therefore, have an important role in setting out what a home is trying to achieve and also in defining the characteristics of the resident group.

Rather to our dismay, however, this documentation proved to be somewhat elusive, and only 5 of the 12 homes had completed Statements of Purpose. To reiterate, this was three years after the legislation required them. Even where Statements existed, we were told on four occasions that this was being revised or was not up to date. The situation in North was better than in South, with four of the five homes able to produce some form of written material. Preparation of this had sometimes taken the form of a staff group exercise, with different individuals delegated to write sections of the Statement, and this had often been considered valuable by the team. The situation varied in private homes but where there was no Statement of Purpose we were referred to publicity information. This was usually quite comprehensive and glossily presented, even replete with crest and Latin motto. Such symbols in themselves suggested a stronger conception of the identity, nature and purpose of the home. However, the publicity of private agencies could also be misleading. In one home the material presented an image of a highly therapeutic environment: on talking to the head of the home it emerged that this was the emphasis of a previous manager and bore little, if any, resemblance to the current work.

The existence of a Statement of Purpose was, however, no guarantee of clarity of aims and objectives. Overall we found Statements in local authority homes to be somewhat bland, lacking guiding principles and with little information regarding methods of work and links with other agencies or the community. Consequently they provided very limited information about the specific populations with which homes envisaged they would be working. It was also often unclear from this documentation how one home differed from another and difficult to compare the exact services that young people would receive. The information we found in the Statements of adolescent homes typically referred to the age group and number of young people catered for, whether stays were intended to be short- or longer term, with some reference made to the reasons why a young person might be looked after in the unit. These homes aimed to provide care and support for the young person, to help enable a return home where appropriate, and to encourage the development of independent living skills. Reference was also made to the need to work in partnership with families and other agencies. This was all rather general and it would seem difficult for the head of any children's home to disagree.

Heads of homes were mostly in agreement with their stated aims but frequently qualified their assent by remarking that they did not match the reality of the current situation. Thus one head of home, while accepting that the unit was intended to operate as a short-term crisis intervention unit for 11–15-year-olds, pointed out that children were often older or younger, had lengthy care histories and spent much more than a short stay at the home. In another facility, undergoing considerable stress, the head of home was even less optimistic, stating that the only current aim was to 'contain and survive'. This hardly augured well for the future development of the home.

The remit for homes for younger children seemed more coherent, though in one of the two units there was again no written Statement. However, the heads of both homes were clear that the units aimed to provide care for children who had experienced considerable disruption in both their family lives and care experience, and to prepare them for new foster carers or rehabilitation with families. One head of home nevertheless noted that while this aim was acceptable, the children now being admitted to the unit presented much more difficult behaviour and in the past would have been directed towards more intensively therapeutic provision. Both homes managed to maintain their boundaries regarding residents' age.

It would not be too much of an exaggeration to conclude that probably only one home fulfilled the criteria of the official guidance regarding the content of its Statement of Purpose. This was the local authority home (I) providing short-term breaks for children with severe learning disabilities. Here the Statement contained a detailed list of aims and objectives, together with information on the methods which would be used to fulfil those aims; including, for example, structured care plans dealing with children's needs regarding feeding routines, physiotherapy and medication. Details of the ways in which staff would engage in social work activities and work with other agencies were also included. This contrasted sharply with the vagueness surrounding methods of work already noted in other local authority homes. Two of the private homes (L and J) were also exceptional in this respect, with both heads of homes and written information making clear that children would have access to counselling and therapy from trained specialists.

Overall, then, the situation regarding Statements of Purpose and Function was disquieting. Yet, as we shall see, the degree to which staff were aware of specific aims and objectives as well as methods of work were important preconditions for homes to operate effectively.

Physical environment

First impressions are important and children's homes have traditionally been renowned for their outwardly stigmatising features. Encouragingly, however, there were relatively few of these to be found and it proved quite difficult to 'spot the children's home'. One clue was usually the large number of staff cars outside, a problem caused by improved staffing ratios. Another give-away feature was often the scratched and battered front door. Where buildings were more stigmatising, such as a home which was part of a social services building, or where the location was very inappropriate, staff and young people were acutely aware of this. Staff in particular felt that a building and the external environment could have a negative effect on morale, and in three homes were therefore keen to move to new locations.

However, children's homes come in all shapes and sizes and it would be difficult to generalise regarding most of their physical features. Any lingering notions of large and gloomy Victorian institutions were soon dashed. We found instead terraced houses in residential neighbourhoods, council houses on large estates and a large villa which had previously functioned as a girls' school.

Buildings were usually in relatively good physical repair and the majority had gardens. Most outwardly attractive was a large farmhouse, located amidst rolling fields. Only three homes were clearly purpose-built and two of these contrived to be relatively pleasant buildings in spite of this. Nine of the 12 homes were in urban areas, two in small towns and one close to a small village; this urban bias is consistent with the Children Act 1989 principle that children be accommodated as far as possible within or close to their own communities. Occasionally we found ironies in location, most notably a home which looked after a number of adolescents with impressive criminal records situated directly opposite the police station.

Interiors can also be stigmatising. Goffman, in his discussion of 'total institutions', commented that stigma could be 'built into' the fabric of a building (Goffman 1968, p.1). This may result from what might be termed 'institutional' furniture or decoration, such as industrial-type kitchen or washing equipment, or alternatively from the way in which space is organised and allocated. In the 1985 study such institutional features included the ringing of the telephone being amplified throughout the building and oversize aluminium teapots that one could barely lift. Noticeable or even excessive damage to the fabric can also be stigmatising. To find oneself in a bedroom where the walls are covered in graffiti undoubtedly highlights the contrast between living with one's family and living in a children's home.

The smaller size of the majority of homes greatly reduced the potential for institutionalisation. Only one home had room for more than ten children and, as we have seen, the average number of residents was six. These small numbers inevitably had implications for the way in which life within the home was experienced and provided scope for a much more 'family-like' atmosphere.

However, some vestiges of the institution remained. Three homes, for example, had entrance lobbies with office-type hatches, which gave the impression of a bureaucratic institution rather than a home and seemed rather unwelcoming. In all homes – interestingly, apart from the two short breaks facilities – there were to be found staff carrying large, jangling bunches of keys. The locking and unlocking of doors and cupboards was thus a regular topic of conversation. The significance attributed to these rituals was suitably captured by one member of staff, who wryly commented that without keys it was impossible to work in the home. The use of keys sometimes seemed to become the essence of the work rather than an incidental feature. Some adolescents even seemed to see staff as synonymous with their keys. But in many homes we also encountered interior decoration and furnishing which helped create a homely atmosphere. Some units would not have been entirely out of place as large family homes, with soft furnishings, lots of photographs and pleasant decoration. This was especially true of the two homes for younger children, where toys, games, pictures, bowls of fruit and cut flowers helped create bright and cheerful environments in which to live.

Adolescent homes tended to incorporate some rather more incongruous features. The video player bolted to the floor with a massive chain is particularly memorable. One home was almost devoid of furniture and lacked television, video and stereo following a spate of damage and theft by residents. In this home, despite the services of a handyman, it was proving difficult to keep up with even everyday repairs: the task was likened to 'painting the Forth Bridge'. Fifty windows had been broken in the month preceding our visit, necessitating special arrangements with a local, prosperous glazier to enable immediate repair. In this home, workmen insisted staff accompany them to ensure their safety. Damage was not, however, always due to vandalism – in one of the short breaks homes, wheelchairs quickly led to damaged paintwork. Other homes struggled with the internal design of their buildings, such as one built for 24 residents which now catered for only six. Chairs and settee stood stranded as an island in the middle of a cavernous living area, and both staff and residents likened this to 'living in a goldfish bowl'.

Upstairs in a children's home the environment was sometimes more institutional, with long rows of doors presenting a forbidding appearance. In research examining the experiences of children living in residential care, issues of privacy have often been prominent (Berridge et al. 1995) and bedrooms are obviously important in providing individual space. Indeed, the majority of children now had their own bedrooms and where these were shared this usually involved siblings. Most homes made arrangements for young people to have keys to their rooms. Of course this may not be any guarantee of security: on the first day of our fieldwork, young people had made a copy of a key providing access to the researcher's room and also his wallet.

Most bedrooms were fairly small, with the exception of one private home where the rooms were quite vast. This home was also notable for the fact that each child had a television and stereo in his or her own bedroom. In homes for adolescents, bedrooms were more likely to be damaged and even to be covered with graffiti. The rapid throughput, one suspects, discourages a more responsible approach. However, many bedrooms were pleasant and had been individually decorated with posters and photographs. Some adolescent girls had created almost replicas of the cosmetics counter at Boots, shrines to self-improvement. Unfortunately, however, the majority of bedrooms did not contain the desk, chair, bookcase and lamp which have been recommended to enable young people to carry out schoolwork (Jackson 1989), although the notion of studying alone was often unpopular.

Daily life

Spending many hours each day in the 12 children's homes provided us with ample opportunity to experience the daily routine. We were especially concerned with those points in the day when young people and staff came together, such as mealtimes or when young people arrived home from school or college, and the nature of the interaction which took place on such occasions. However, the way in which staff spent their time when young people were absent was also of interest. Routines sometimes varied according to the type of home but, on the whole, the daily life of the homes proved very similar and, by the conclusion of the fieldwork, the researchers found it relatively easy to slot into this.

The atmosphere in the majority of homes was pleasant and friendly. This was reflected in our experience as researchers – we were almost invariably made to feel welcome and comfortable (if, on two occasions following thefts, being a few pounds worse off!). In homes for younger children there was inevitably more activity and noise. Only one home (E) emanated a noticeable atmosphere of tension. Even here, however, the situation varied according to the group of staff on duty. Otherwise relationships between staff were generally good and were often characterised by much laughter and good humour: essential ingredients of residential work. In North the links between staff working in different homes were especially positive and there were frequent phone calls to and fro.

Even on occasions when the atmosphere was somewhat frenetic, the relationships between staff and young people were consistently good. Tensions were frequently dissipated by joking and teasing. Staff were always addressed by their first names and were highly approachable. While, as we shall see, staff voiced concerns over methods of control and restraint, no such fears were apparent in regard to the display of affection and we observed frequent public, wholly appropriate hugs, cuddles and other forms of physical reassurance. It is sometimes claimed that staff are afraid of any physical contact with children, and that the latter freely make unwarranted allegations, but we found no evidence of this whatsoever.

It is important to appreciate that young people clearly enjoyed being with staff and continually sought their company. Individual time spent with keyworkers was also highly valued. Attempts to keep young people out of 'the office' were consequently fraught with difficulty. In one home (E), where the atmosphere was especially crisis-ridden, staff were extremely protective of their space and used the office essentially as a refuge from the resident group. This was deeply resented and young people continually sought, by fair means or foul, to break through this barrier. In other homes the staff smoking room or the kitchen provided the focal point of interaction. As Millham *et al.* (1979) emphasised in their study of approved schools, it is not young people who avoid contact with staff but the opposite.

We did not undertake a detailed study of subcultural behaviour in homes, but our evidence would support other research, also using participant observation, which found such subcultures to be weak among young people (and staff) (Brown *et al.* forthcoming). Subcultures are, however, by their very nature difficult to penetrate. Another study of residential care has indicated that the extent of bullying and exploitation, for example, is much greater than is generally appreciated (Sinclair and Gibbs 1996). Interactions between children with severe learning disabilities in group care also seem to be very much unexplored, both conceptually and empirically.

For young people it seems likely that the weakness of subculture is at least partly due to the fact that the period of residence is generally short. It may also be that self-centredness among emotionally deprived or disruptive children hinders strong, enduring peer relationships. In three homes (F, G and L) we observed or were told about bullying; in each case staff were aware of this and in one home children reported the problem at group meetings. In the homes for younger children, where sexual abuse featured in the backgrounds of the majority of young people, staff were also extremely conscious of the dangers of sexualised behaviour between peers.

Where subcultures did exist among young people, these tended to operate more in relation to social networks *outside* the home. They were consequently impossible to observe. For most of our adolescent homes, networks had developed with care leavers who continued to live locally. In North the result of this seemed to be that young people, especially females, were placed at risk. In one home (C) a girl had been pressurised into sexual relationships with older men by other female residents in the home. Staff also complained that groups of youths loitered near the home. This was difficult to control, despite the co-operation of police in the area. In another home such networks were reported to have led to young people becoming involved with drugs.

Homes for adolescents were unexpectedly quiet during the day. Where the buildings were large, young people and staff dispersed and it could be difficult for the researcher eagerly clutching interview schedules to find members of either group. In such homes we found few residents attending school and the researcher often arrived before young people had emerged from bed. Later in the day residents would vanish to unknown destinations, supposedly to visit relatives but more probably to hang around the local shopping centre. Others sat watching television or accompanied staff on errands. One irritating young man spent two hours banging out 'Greensleeves' on a keyboard. Most adolescents who were not attending school appeared bored or lethargic but occasionally there was more active discontent. In one home young people continually banged on the office door, demanding to know what was planned for them, and justifiably expressed frustration over the fact that there was little structure to the day.

In homes for younger children and those offering short-term breaks, the day seemed more clearly organised, mainly as a result of the larger number of children attending school. Consequently the early morning saw staff organising dinner money and ensuring that children had everything they needed. Children in the two short breaks homes had to be ready to leave from 8 o'clock and staff would work from 6.30 a.m. to ensure all the children were waiting for their buses and taxis. This part of the day was therefore extremely pressurised in such homes, especially in view of the fact that several staff were sometimes required to bath and dress a child. The subsequent lull was, however, abruptly ended at half past three when the group would reappear *en masse*. From then on there would be constant activity. As one member of staff in a home for younger children remarked, 'you have to be a full-time entertainer in this job'. Recovering from yet another unaccustomed game of football, we could well appreciate the demands on the energy and imagination of the staff group.

In all homes the activities of staff during the day seemed fairly similar. The shift pattern inevitably introduces structure to the day and, as the 1985 study observed, there was much preoccupation with the staffing rota. The organisation of this usually transcended the comprehension of the researcher, as shifts were continually rearranged. Young people, however, often displayed an adept understanding of these complex patterns of organisation. One interesting situation arose when the four-year-old, introduced in the previous chapter, was put to bed by her keyworker. However, on being unable to sleep and calling for attention at 3 a.m., was faced with a *different* member of staff who entered her room. 'Confusing isn't it, love?', commented the substitute at breakfast in something of an understatement.

In local authorities staff were sometimes exchanged between homes. The shift patterns also varied among different categories of establishment. In the two short breaks homes, for example, there were night- as well as day-staff. Some children had to be woken and turned at regular intervals. There were also night monitors (communication devices) in each room in case someone needed attention. In two of the private homes, staff were usually expected to work longer shifts than was the case in local authorities – in one home 24-hour shifts had been introduced. Other homes followed more standard patterns, but even here circumstances sometimes resulted in the same two or three members of staff being on duty for the majority of the researcher's visit.

Shifts were broken by the ubiquitous handover meeting, when staff were updated on the happenings of the preceding eight hours and issues arising in regard to individual children. Handovers served a variety of social functions within the home, providing staff whose shift was completed with the opportunity to unburden themselves, while those who had just arrived would be prepared for the hours ahead. In this sense these meetings, however much interrupted by the ringing of the telephone, could be an oasis in the midst of a hectic and harassing day. While some children would knock on the office door throughout, it was noticeable that they generally respected the sanctity of the handover and accepted this as a justifiable reason for the temporary absence of staff. Expectations of acceptable behaviour, therefore, can be developed. In one short breaks home (I) the handover was also instrumental in offering all staff in turn, regardless of status, the opportunity to lead the meeting, write up the notes and pass on information. Each shift also appointed a lead fire officer. Neither of these practices was planned in the other 11 homes, though the former sometimes happened by default.

Throughout the day staff were engaged in a range of administrative tasks, including writing reports and updating log books. Contact had to be made with social workers and occasionally with schools and other agencies. Considerable energy went into planning activities – for example, in one private home a holiday was being organised during our visit. However, in adolescent homes especially, the day tended to proceed in a more leisurely fashion, interrupted by numerous breaks for the cups of strong tea required by residential social workers. Our field notes for one home record that 'the pace is usually relaxed'. This was often understandable where staff had been dealing with young people into the early hours of the morning and were physically exhausted. The situation was somewhat different in private homes, where staff were more likely to have responsibility for cooking and even cleaning, and where staff ratios also tended to be lower (see Chapter 6).

Evening activities were an important part of the day in almost all the children's homes we visited. As in the 1985 study, staff sometimes had mixed views on the number of activities offered to young people, feeling that they could raise unrealistic expectations and make parents, often unable to provide similar opportunities, feel inadequate. At the same time, it was recognised that wider experiences were important in developing young people's outlook and social skills, while demonstrating the availability of alternative forms of entertainment. In the case of adolescents who had spent rather sedentary days, the activities could also be used to work off surplus energy. Most outings involved visits to the cinema or to leisure centres and were usually enjoyed by staff and young people alike. For researchers, however, being dragged around a roller rink by energetic 15-year-olds is rarely included in standard texts on participant observation.

Such outings fulfilled an additional function in homes offering short-term breaks for disabled children. These placements often provided a relatively rare opportunity for young people to socialise with other children outside the school context. Parents could find it difficult to arrange outings in the absence of suitable transport and help, and we know that they welcome age-appropriate relevant activities for children (Russell 1996). Staff felt that some children were consequently very isolated and understimulated. Alongside its shortcomings, residential care, nonetheless, has certain advantages over family life. Staff in the two short breaks homes thus viewed social activities as a crucial part of care programmes and made considerable efforts, including long and difficult journeys, to take children to places of interest. One home, for example, had recently participated in the London 'Strollerthon' and had travelled to Birmingham for a recording of *Gladiators*, as well as a holiday to Butlins. Children seemed eager to go out at every opportunity and the minibus filled at a few minutes' notice. In one home, while aware of its charitable overtones, staff seemed to have an endless supply of free tickets to shows and concerts.

Fieldwork in the two short breaks homes yielded much insight into the nature of disability in our society. It was clear that major problems for those involved stemmed from external social and physical barriers as well as their own impairments (Hales 1996; Oliver 1990). Equipment could be old, inefficient or unreliable: a lift in one home broke down for 24 hours and a young woman requiring a wheelchair was stranded upstairs. Securing wheelchairs in a minibus was time-consuming and problematic. Uneven pavements, kerbs and inconveniently parked cars posed formidable obstacles. Social attitudes were equally exclusive. Parents beckoned away their offspring from a disabled child on a swing, as if in fear of contamination. Members of the public stared. A child with cerebral palsy enjoyed the cinema but made involuntary noises when excited. 'Can't you shut that kid up?' a member of the audience shouted angrily. 'Shut up yourself!' retaliated his keyworker. Staff were not convinced that advances in health care had been equally matched by social progress.

At the end of the day, bedtimes were perhaps the subject of less conflict than might have been expected. All homes had fairly strict rules regarding age-appropriate bedtimes. While there were inevitable objections and attempts to cajole staff into extending these, children quite frequently admitted to being tired and occasionally even asked to go to bed. The clear line thus paid dividends. Bedtimes for younger children were usually handled well. Children liked to be put to bed by an individual member of staff and were often read to. Adolescents unsurprisingly posed the greatest problems and bedtimes ranked among their most frequent complaints. Many adolescents complained of sleeping badly and looked tired in the mornings. Some of this may have been attributable to something worrying them or depression, but we encountered little discussion of how adolescents had slept and what could be done about it. Certainly, on the three occasions it occurred, neither researcher found sleeping in a children's home to be restful. There was much noise from downstairs, corridors and neighbouring rooms as well as the plumbing system. For us as temporary residents, two of these three homes felt poorly designed and built. Sound proofing was ineffective. Lack of sleep is a serious issue in view of the educational problems of many children looked after, and it is unlikely that children will concentrate well if they have slept badly.

Food and mealtimes

Social scientists, especially anthropologists, have traditionally drawn attention to the importance of 'commensality', or collective eating, in forging and sustaining social relationships (Douglas 1975; Mennell, Murcott and van Otterloo 1992). This has been recognised in official guidance and other texts on residential child care which have advised that, wherever possible, children have access to kitchens and share in the preparation of food (Department of Health 1991b). One practice text adds that, 'it is impossible to create a good living environment if children and young people do not enjoy their food' (Kahan 1994, p.83). Not only is this an important social activity but practical skills in cooking are important to young people's development.

The social significance of food and eating was certainly evident in homes, where the kitchen was often the focal point of the building and the most homely room in the house. On the researcher's arrival at one home, several children and most of the staff were to be found congenially occupied in making large, unhealthy, delicious fried egg sandwiches. During a preliminary visit to an adolescent unit, one (male) resident had prepared a plate of home-made scones with cream and jam. Indeed, in a number of homes young people contributed to the cooking and clearly enjoyed this. These incidents are notable for the contribution they made to the atmosphere of homes and the opportunity for young people to share in them was undoubtedly valuable. Yet the degree to which children were permitted access to the kitchen and to food varied considerably. The preparation of snacks in the evenings by staff also contributed to the creation of a 'family-like' atmosphere and children appreciated being given treats before bedtime. It was noticeable that young people who stayed out late often returned earlier if particular staff were working and they had something planned, including perhaps a tasty and imaginative late night snack. It would be inappropriate here to go into the issue of diet in any detail beyond the general observation that food was always plentiful although, overall, there was a lack of fresh fruit and vegetables.

For our research, mealtimes often proved a critical guide in gauging social interactions and the atmosphere of the home during that day. As in the majority of families, some mealtimes were characterised by considerable tension and could forewarn conflict later in the day or night. But most mealtimes were enjoyable, as staff and young people talked companionably together. Occasionally awkwardness resulted from institutional arrangements, such as the home where there were insufficient chairs for young people, staff and the researcher. The structure of meals tended to vary according to the type of home. In one of the homes for younger children, meals were frequently noisy and messy. Here, conflicts between children were also frequent, sometimes breaking out into fights. These were difficult to predict and prevent. Staff usually worked hard to encourage children to eat and also to correct table manners, but sometimes had to be content with maintaining control. Similarly, in the two homes for children with severe learning disabilities, meals may have appeared disorderly to onlookers. However, here we found mealtimes to assume a different and more positive significance, in that teaching a child to eat, use cutlery or develop social skills was often an important part of the child's care plan. Helping a disabled child to eat could also be time-consuming for staff, for example in one case taking a worker two hours to feed one child.

Adolescent homes displayed a more casual approach to eating. This partly reflects adolescent routines and should not necessarily be viewed as negative. However, in one home it was also a reflection of the general lack of structure, as young people wandered in, removed food from the table, then vanished. In two homes the significance of mealtimes was reduced by the fact that some residents were on 'independence' training and cooked for themselves. This arrangement was not always a happy one; it could be difficult to enjoy a substantial and nutritious meal while two members of the group sat down to another plate of unappetising noodles.

Care for specific groups

As we showed in the previous chapter, the residents of our 12 children's homes were a diverse group with a wide range of needs. Many had experienced considerable stress within their families, presented behavioural difficulties and had health problems. While it was difficult to categorise children, particularly adolescents, we did explore whether the needs of certain groups were being met within the homes – specifically girls, children from minority ethnic groups and care leavers. Each of these areas would obviously merit more detailed investigation but it could be useful to raise at least some issues based on our fieldwork.

We have already shown that girls outnumbered boys in both adolescent and short breaks homes. In three homes the converse applied, with a much higher proportion of boys than girls. There are a number of care issues which are especially pertinent for girls, including the allocation of gender roles within the home; whether potential abuse issues are recognised by staff; and, less tangibly, whether the atmosphere within a home is noticeably 'masculine'. Heads of homes tended to demonstrate a much greater awareness of these issues than other staff, often raising such matters independently during interviews. The reactions of staff to questions about care for young women were rather less positive: the majority looked blank and several laughed. In two homes it seemed to us that girls were at risk of sexual exploitation by male residents – these were not simply 'normal' adolescent relationships. These dangers were most prominent in one unit where young people had formed networks outside the home. These appeared to include older men. As has already been noted, in one home an adolescent girl had been placed at risk by the placement, during which she was pressurised into sexual activity by other (female) residents. The placement of girls who had experienced sexual abuse in homes where there was a high proportion of male residents was also questionable: this applied probably to two of our five adolescent homes. Staff in one home acknowledged that social workers would place girls there only if they were 'at the end of their tether'. Specific issues relating to gender were raised in homes caring for disabled children. Some parents had requested that their daughters were given personal care only by female members of staff. Although the gender balance of shifts sometimes made it difficult, both homes operated this policy.

Encouragingly, we uncovered relatively little gender stereotyping in terms of household roles. Boys were encouraged to share in household chores and sexist remarks were challenged. In most homes the gender balance of the staff group helped to provide positive role models and male staff were involved in cooking meals and cleaning.

The issue of care for minority ethnic groups was often perceived to be somewhat irrelevant, as many homes were located in areas where the minority ethnic population was small. However, this does not detract from the need to develop anti-racist attitudes among young people and, indeed, staff in a number of homes expressed concern at the extent of prejudice among the resident group. We also know from educational research that racist behaviour is more likely to occur in settings where minority ethnic pupils are small in number (Troyna and Hatcher 1992). As shown in the previous chapter, all but 1 of the 12 children from minority ethnic groups were from Borough and were living in private homes (7) or the one offering short breaks (4). In one home in North, however, young people were taken for a Chinese meal to celebrate Chinese New Year and this seemed a very positive example of an attempt to raise cultural awareness. In another home in the same authority, staff training on the issue had taken place and a list had been compiled of, for example, food stores and places of worship appropriate to different ethnic groups. South, in contrast, had given anti-racism less attention.

Staff in the two private homes in virtually all-white areas were sometimes rather defensive about the placement there of minority ethnic children, and were anxious to demonstrate their capacity to cater for the needs of these young people. We did observe some good practice taking place in these settings, for example in regard to skin and hair care. One eight-year-old was extremely proud of her hair cream and comb and frequently informed her fellow residents that she had 'special' hair. In the one private (L) and one short breaks home (I), where the minority ethnic population of the surrounding area was greater, we found more African-Caribbean staff. In these homes cultural needs were given greater attention and became an integral part of care practices. For example, African-Caribbean meals were often on the menu, different styles of music were heard, children were taken shopping in black areas, translation facilities were provided for non-English-speaking parents, and in one case a befriender had been involved in helping a young person address issues related to his cultural identity. Another memorable example was of a Chinese girl with no mobility, speech or vision, for whom staff played tapes of stories in Chinese at night as she drifted to sleep. This is an example of good practice in a field which has been criticised for being insufficiently sensitive to the needs of different communities (Department of Health Social Services Inspectorate 1994b).

Only two of the homes for adolescents made specific provision for young people aged 16 or above, but older adolescents lived in several of the other homes we visited. In most adolescent homes residents were involved in carrying out household chores and were responsible for their own washing and ironing. Many also enjoyed the opportunity to cook meals. However, although staff talked about the need to teach young people about budgeting and to encourage a more realistic view of living alone, we observed few examples of this taking place. Only one home (K) had active links with employers. This was a private home where the staff had various contacts in the local area which they had used to provide young people with work experience on a local building site and garage. In most homes preparation for leaving care also seemed to be viewed as something which could take place over the last few months of a young person's residence rather than being integrated into their care plan. Staff usually recognised the inadequacy of existing arrangements but, nevertheless, the amount of preparation being provided for adolescents of all ages was very disappointing.

In particular, preparation for 'independence' seemed very much *ad hoc* and seldom were staff working to a planned structured programme. Furthermore, there still was a strong tendency to concentrate on practical skills and to overlook social and personal issues, such as coping with isolation, loneliness and depression or how to make and sustain friends (Stein and Carey 1986). This is alarming in view of the poor prognosis for many care leavers, including unemployment, mental health problems and involvement in criminal activities (Biehal *et al.* 1994; Carlen, Gleeson and Wardhaugh 1992; Cheung and Heath 1994; Devlin 1996; Strathdee and Johnson 1994).

Behavioural control

A number of public inquiries have taken place into children's homes in recent years, focusing on the inappropriate use of methods of behavioural control, resulting in serious abuse. Perhaps most notorious was the Pindown regime in Staffordshire, in which children were confined to barely furnished rooms for long periods, deprived of external contact and required to wear night clothes during the day (Levy and Kahan 1991). While the circumstances giving rise to abusive regimes in children's homes are complex, various shortcomings associated with inadequate management, policy and practice have been identified (Berridge and Brodie 1996; Jones 1994, 1995). Where certain conditions exist, there is clearly much greater potential for individuals to use their positions of power to abuse the children in their care.

Consequently, in response to the scandals which have taken place in residential care, Department of Health (1993, 1997) guidance and other initiatives (Department of Health 1996d) have sought to address a range of management and practice issues and so to improve performance in the sector as a whole.

Behavioural control was undoubtedly a major preoccupation in all of the homes we visited. This is unsurprising in that, as we have already shown, some two-thirds of our sample of residents had previously presented serious behavioural problems at home, school or in the community. 'Control' was the single issue about which staff expressed greatest concern in their work. It was also the area in which they had received most training: the majority reported that they had attended in-house training sessions on matters concerning control and restraint. This included the private sector, where less training took place overall. Nevertheless, the majority of staff, with the notable exception of the two short breaks homes, expressed the view that they encountered major control problems in their work. Many complained that they found Department of Health guidance on the issue confusing and restrictive. Several also claimed that they were disadvantaged by the emphasis on 'children's rights' and that young people now had effectively more rights than did staff.

Though to a certain degree it could be argued that staff were ill-informed about certain issues, they acknowledged that it was not so much that they did not know what they should be doing but that a theoretical understanding of effective measures of control was not being translated into practice. Staff often remarked, especially in South, that a major explanation for their passivity was that, should they physically confront a young person who subsequently made an allegation, they would not feel confident that they would be supported, or even treated fairly, by local authority management.

These views contrasted with the attitudes of staff in the two homes for children with severe learning disabilities, where remarkably little concern was expressed regarding behavioural control. This was perhaps surprising given that children in these two centres often displayed extremely difficult and disruptive behaviour, including violent tantrums, climbing on cupboards and bookshelves and removing clothing. When these problems occurred, staff usually responded promptly, firmly and consistently, making clear to children when their behaviour was unacceptable. Behavioural control in these two homes was often addressed in individual care plans. Interestingly, at the end of shifts, staff in these two homes also did *not* dwell on the behavioural management problems and, in despair, lose sight of wider care objectives.

The uncertainty which staff felt was reflected in sometimes passive attitudes to young people's behaviour. There were a number of episodes where a situation was potentially explosive but where no preventive action was taken, or where an incident seemed to be mishandled. This was especially noticeable in homes where there was a higher number of physical restraints. In total, in our 54 days' fieldwork we observed 12 restraints, involving 8 children. Unexpectedly, more of these involved younger children rather than adolescents, and there were more females than males. One 13-year-old girl in South became uncontrollable when told that a child protection conference concerning her was due to be held in an hour and a half, at which she was expected to attend. The recommendation was to be that she be moved to a secure unit as part of the protection plan. The meeting had been arranged over several days but it was decided not to tell her in case she ran away. Two other cases of restraint in South involved young women with a history of abuse, which seemed to have a direct relationship to their behaviour. These incidents appeared to be fairly predictable but no forethought occurred. In fact, in only one (private) home (K) did we find staff that operated a planned strategy concerning incidents of misbehaviour.

Control problems affecting adolescents mostly concerned their desire to leave the building, rather than conflict and disagreement in the home itself. In most adolescent homes, young people were not prevented from going out late at night in situations that seemed to us to contain risks. This included unaccompanied young women. Three of the adolescent homes in North, in particular, were in environments which were acknowledged to be unsafe.

Some homes had certainly experienced serious incidents concerning young people's behaviour. In one (E), there had been a series of attacks on staff just prior to the researcher's visit, together with numerous thefts and considerable damage to the home. Staff in this establishment had almost given up on any attempt to control young people's behaviour. This was illustrated by the bizarre actions of the residential social worker who methodically knocked the glass from all the picture frames 'before the residents do it'. In another home one young person had recently died and another had been seriously injured following a joy-riding incident. Where staff had experienced such extreme difficulties it was unsurprising that morale and confidence should be affected. However, it was still a matter of concern that staff felt unable to act to control, and even to protect, young people.

Yet in many respects the number of observable incidents related to control were fewer than might have been expected. Many episodes were minor and skilfully dealt with, such as pocket money disputes, arguments over clothing and so on. Young people mostly responded positively to requests from staff to alter their behaviour. Sanctions were fairly standard – paying for damages from pocket money or, in the case of younger children, going to bed slightly earlier. Unacceptable behaviour was usually, but not always, challenged verbally. On some occasions more formal methods of control were instituted: for example, in one home for younger children (G), meetings were held with the children to discuss issues of behaviour ('naughty meetings'). Adolescents would readily, when asked, take their dirty shoes and boots off chairs, remove baseball caps at the meal table and clear away dirty plates and cups. They would almost always (eventually) help when asked to assist with a task. There are hundreds of such events each day in a children's home. Our observations, therefore, indicated that staff often exercised effective control but were unaware of the success of their interventions. With adolescents, they were also reluctant to impose boundaries when it really mattered. Indeed, our discussions with adolescents often revealed that they expected more control than they actually received.

Family contact

A key finding of research leading up to the Children Act 1989 was the inadequacy of existing arrangements for contact between children looked after and their families (Department of Health and Social Security 1985; Millham *et al.* 1986). Families received little help and support over visiting and a number of barriers to contact were identified. These included restrictions resulting from distance and unwelcoming attitudes on the part of residential staff (and foster carers), as well as the more specific limits placed on the access of certain family members to a young person. At the same time, it was demonstrated that the majority of children looked after returned home, usually after a short period away. Where contact is sustained such returns are usually both more swift and successful (Bullock *et al.* 1993). The Children Act 1989 subsequently sought to address these concerns, taking the important step of making 'partnership with parents' one of the main principles of the legislation. Increased contact between children and their parents was also to be facilitated by placing children if possible within their own communities.

Obviously the issue of contact is not a straightforward one. Children have usually left their homes following some sort of crisis and relationships will often be seriously damaged. Some children will be looked after as a result of abuse and contact with certain family members may be undesirable or dangerous. Many parents are rejecting, unco-operative and refuse to accept at least some responsibility. Households may also undergo a change in membership during the young person's residence in a children's home, potentially unsettling relationships and making contact more difficult to sustain (Millham *et al.* 1986). However, it is now widely accepted that for the majority of children, maintaining contact with families is a crucial aspect of promoting a child's welfare and ultimately in facilitating their return home.

Staff in the 12 homes overwhelmingly reflected these views and were positive about helping children maintain and improve their relationships with their families. In all the homes we visited we found children phoning their parents and other family members. These calls were followed up by staff, who mostly were well informed about children's families and their circumstances. Parents also phoned the home: for example, to see if a child had returned safely from a scout camp. However, considerable sensitivity was also required. Most adolescents had experienced some form of family rejection and, even where the young person was anxious to renew contact, this was not always reciprocated. In other cases young people themselves were reluctant to make contact and had to be encouraged to do so. Staff tried hard to work with young people on these issues and were encouraged at any evidence of commitment on the part of parents, such as attending a review. Apart from its intrinsic merits, it was also recognised that the re-establishment of family contact was often crucial in view of the absence of alternative placements for adolescents.

Among younger children, child protection issues were prominent and some were subject to court orders limiting the amount of contact they might have with parents. In such cases, staff encouraged contact with siblings and grandparents or, in some cases, with former foster carers. Younger children tended to talk more about their families and to produce photographs which they were anxious to show the researchers. Where home visits were possible – in one unit there was almost an exodus at weekends – staff were careful to monitor children's reactions on their return. Aside from issues of abuse or rejection, distance also constituted a major barrier to contact. This mainly applied to private homes. Staff were always willing to transport young people but this could create pressures on other staff within a home.

As with the 1985 study, visits to the children's home by residents' families were still very rare. In our 54 days' fieldwork we encountered only seven parents. In North this was partly due to the fact that young people lived so close to their families that they preferred to make the visits and these sometimes occurred on a daily basis. In one centre, staff also tried to visit the young person's home and to hold meetings there as a means of involving families in the social work programme. The absence of suitable facilities, specifically the lack of a free room where families could meet in a relaxed atmosphere, was also an important factor in most homes, especially as they are now smaller. But major elements also are social and psychological obstacles. Parents can feel guilty, insecure and confused. Other aspects of their lives may also be in crisis, particularly as separation is likely to have occurred relatively recently, thus influencing the degree of attention sons and daughters receive. In some cases, parents and new partners may also be rather ambivalent about the future relationship, especially where the child has been problematic in the past. An example of good practice was one private home where support for parents was built into the care package. This was an imaginative approach which seemed to work well. For example, one parent that we met visited the home frequently and was given advice on parenting skills by staff, as well as having the opportunity to talk and play with her two children. She was clearly comfortable and relaxed within the children's home and seemed to enjoy the company of staff. Unfortunately this practice was very rare.

Teatime visits by parents and siblings also took place to one of the short breaks homes. Generally, here, the contact issues for children living away from home were rather different. Most staff viewed the experience as providing a much needed break for parents as well as for children. More liaison between staff and parents, therefore, tended to take place outside the actual period of short-term care. Understandably many parents found it initially difficult to use the service and required reassurance and support from staff in taking this step. They had often struggled on for long periods and typically experienced feelings of guilt and failure at being unable to cope alone. Parents may have preferred family-based short-term care, though this was unavailable. There seems a particular dearth of minority ethnic short-term carers (Robinson 1996a). Residential staff and other services also worked with parents in order to implement the child's care plan. However, there was a degree of tension over whether parents should make contact while the child was away. This is linked to the issue of for whom exactly is the short break provided, although children have been positive about the experience (Robinson *et al.* 1994). Parents were welcomed when they visited but not made to feel uncomfortable if they did not. Nevertheless, unresolved tensions existed in relation to this issue in the short breaks homes.

Community links

Current legislation and good practice emphasise that, as far as possible, children should be placed within their local communities. The potential advantages of this are clear: the trauma of separation is lessened, contact with parents and other family members is facilitated, and children are enabled to continue to attend existing schools. With the exception of two of the three private homes, and to a lesser extent the two homes for adolescents in South, the children's homes we visited were of the type implied by the Children Act 1989 and the majority of children were thus living near their communities.

The benefits of encouraging children to participate in the life of the community were clear. Younger children in particular were involved in a full programme of activities, including football, gymnastics, cubs and scouts. Staff in these homes were constantly seeking out new interests for residents and worked hard to encourage them to attend. Membership of clubs or youth groups was much rarer amongst the more restless adolescents but there were some notable exceptions, such as the enthusiastic basket-ball player. One young person remanded to an adolescent home was learning to play the piano. Children in all types of home used local leisure facilities, though the residents from one private home had been banned from the local cinema. Children also sometimes had friends living locally, though this was more apparent in North than in South or the private homes. One home for younger children had forged especially positive links with their immediate neighbours and young people constantly played with other children and went to tea with them. It was, however, much more difficult for children to invite friends to a residential unit: we noted only one such visit during our observations, which did not turn out well due to the embarrassment caused by some other residents. This corresponded with the general lack of visitors, adults or children, to the homes and made our presence novel for both young people and staff. Thus, as in the previous study, adolescent children's homes especially continue to be curiously socially isolated institutions. Their physical location in neighbourhoods, paradoxically, makes this worse. This is added to by the fact that staff now no longer live in. For the researcher, the sense of 'social disconnectedness' after living in a children's home for four days was very significant.

Integration into the community, however, is not necessarily positive. In North children usually had close relationships with their communities but these were often negative and frequently placed children at risk of involvement in criminal and promiscuous activities. The community-oriented approach to residential care depicted in the Children Act 1989, therefore, may not be appropriate for persistent delinquents with local subcultures. The television set was stolen from one home in North by removing sufficient bricks from the outside wall. Problems also resulted from the hostile attitudes of many neighbourhoods to the notion of having a children's home in their midst. This was reflected in the major difficulties encountered by social services departments in all the areas we visited when trying to locate new premises for children's homes. Indeed, it was refreshing to be told by the new cook in one private home that few people in the nearby village were aware that the house was a children's home.

The prevailing local view, most residential staff told us, was that these were dangerous children likely to cause trouble (short breaks homes excepted). In some instances these fears had been justified and surrounding properties and cars had been damaged by young people. One such mercurial episode occurred, remarkably, during a cigarette break at half-time in watching the video of *Bambi*. In such cases staff were sympathetic to neighbours and would try to make amends: for example, in a home for younger children, letters of apology had been delivered to neighbours following a series of broken windows. Despite all this, we would have no qualms about living next door to 10 of these 12 homes, perhaps the ultimate evaluation.

As one might expect, hostility was greatest in regard to adolescents. This was reflected in the experience of a home for younger children, on moving to a new site, which had found that antagonism was significantly diminished when the age group of residents was made clear. Some homes had suffered from extremely adverse publicity, which was clearly damaging to the morale of both staff and residents. One adolescent unit featured prominently in the local newspaper throughout the researcher's stay, and even had its own Teletext page dedicated to it. Regrettably, however, the hostility which existed in other communities seemed to derive more from prevailing media images regarding children's homes than any specific behaviour on the part of young people. One group of residents wrote to the local newspaper in frustration. Some staff spoke nostalgically of a more charitable era when neighbours were more likely to view residents as needy rather than undeserving, which was the relationship the two short breaks homes had painstakingly managed to develop in their own communities.

Links with other agencies

Our consideration of the important area of the links between a children's home and the wider world encompassed relationships with other professionals. In recent years it has been increasingly recognised that effective social work and residential care practice are dependent on positive relationships and joint working with other agencies. This has been reflected in, for example, policies and procedures in child protection which make explicit such inter-agency practice (Home Office *et al.* 1991). The complex backgrounds and range of difficulties which many young people entering residential placements have experienced also makes such joint working imperative. However, this is an area which is often beset with problems (Audit Commission 1994). It has been noted that legislation introduced in other areas, such as education, is in important respects incompatible with the philosophy on which the Children Act 1989 is based (Jones and Bilton 1994; Sinclair, Garnett and Berridge 1995). Consequently agencies may be working to different agendas. Where a young person requires the help of more than one service, the failure to define roles or allocate responsibility adequately may prevent needs from being addressed. Research has demonstrated that this may ultimately lead to a number of young people, usually adolescents, falling through the net of all welfare services. And though we all endorse that inter-professional collaboration is essential, there seem to be some quite fundamental structural inhibitions to it occurring in practice (Roaf and Lloyd 1995).

The range of agencies which might be involved with a young person is obviously too great to permit examination of all the potential contacts. We therefore confined our observations to the links which existed between the children's home and health services, police and, in social services, fieldworkers and fostering services. Links with education services, a major issue, will be considered at the end of this chapter as part of the wider discussion of schooling.

Of these groups, the most positive link, interestingly, was overwhelmingly that with police. This was an unexpected finding but applied to homes of all types in each of the areas we visited. Even more fascinatingly, young people and staff alike spoke positively of contact with community policemen and women and it is significant that during our fieldwork we observed more visits from police than from any other external agency. In one home the community policeman had organised a weekend skating trip for the group and, in another, to play pool with some of the young people. Staff felt that the police were extremely tolerant in many situations, specifically when they were required to report that a child had not returned to the home after a specific time. The young person often reappeared shortly afterwards but police were usually good humoured about the extra paperwork involved and appreciated the local regulations under which residential social workers were operating. Police also responded promptly on occasions when a young person had unexpectedly taken off and staff were particularly concerned about their welfare, as we were able to observe twice during our visits. More frustrating, perhaps, were the frequent hoax emergency phone calls placed by one seven-year-old – one of which occurred embarrassingly, and to our amazement, during our interview with her.

Rather ironically, the relationships which staff reported with police were not replicated within social services, and the quality of the links which existed with social workers was much more variable. Indeed, an important and disconcerting finding was that staff generally reported better relationships with external professionals than with social workers. In part this seemed to be related to the traditional gap in status between fieldworkers and residential social workers, which was felt to have been exacerbated by purchaser–provider organisational splits. Staff occasionally complained that they were perceived as a 'baby-sitting' service by fieldworkers. There was also a sense that fieldworkers failed to listen to or acknowledge the fact that residential staff also had considerable expertise regarding a child's day-to-day behaviour. In one home staff recounted triumphantly a recent incident when a fieldworker had left the children's home physically shaking following a meeting with a young person. They felt that prior to this incident she had not appreciated the challenge this individual presented. However, the main complaints of residential social workers concerned lack of information. Private homes were particularly frustrated by the difficulties of making contact with social workers and had found that these problems tended to apply to specific local authorities. Where long distances were involved there were complaints regarding the rarity of visits from fieldworkers.

Nevertheless, staff spoke appreciatively of individual examples of work that fieldworkers had carried out with young people. We observed a number of such visits to children's homes: in one home three social workers visited over a period of three days, including the weekend. Interactions in these cases were always amicable. In North, the short breaks home for disabled children had recently transferred from adult to children's services, and since this had taken place staff felt that their relationships with fieldworkers had noticeably improved. In the Borough equivalent, close links existed with the children's disability team and some residential staff had been seconded to this. Indeed, a number of important fieldwork tasks, including co-ordinating work with other agencies, were handed over to residential staff in both short breaks homes and this had led to some positive practice. For example, residential staff often assumed greater responsibility for maintaining links with health and education services than was the case in other children's homes. The outcome was that roles and responsibilities seemed more clearly demarcated.

Children's homes also potentially had links with fostering services. This varied according to the category of home. In units catering for adolescents, where fostering was usually felt to be an impractical option, we found little evidence of active partnerships. The situation was very different in homes for younger children. Although the young people living in these placements had often experienced a number of failed fostering placements, it was often still intended that another long-term family placement be found. Staff were committed to this goal and, interestingly, we found a number of residential social workers in these homes who were foster carers themselves. In one case the head of home was a member of the fostering panel. Such links clearly helped facilitate positive relationships. In both North and South there was a serious shortage of foster carers who were considered appropriate for young children in these homes, and they often had to wait for lengthy periods before a suitable placement could be found. In one home, three of the children – a four-year-old and two brothers aged 11 and 12 – had been waiting for two years. While staff were frustrated by this, and sometimes expressed anger at the effect of such delays on young people, most were aware of the problems associated with recruiting foster carers and did not hold the fostering service responsible for these shortcomings. This is part of a wider problem (Association of Directors of Social Services 1997; Berridge 1997).

Health

Good parenting clearly requires due attention to the health and health education needs of young people. Where children have experienced disadvantage, these needs are often more acute. However, the health of children in care has generally been a neglected issue (Brodie *et al.* 1997; Ward 1995), which hopefully the *Looking After Children* planning package will now help to remedy (Department of Health 1995b). Children have frequently failed to receive appropriate inoculations or health checks, and health education has tended to be given a low priority. We were therefore interested in finding out how much awareness of health issues existed among staff and whether there were positive relationships with local health professionals.

In most cases such links had a fairly low profile. The majority of children were registered with local GPs and dentists and, during our visits, we observed appointments being made and children being encouraged and enabled to attend. Where children were living within their own communities, they usually remained on the register of the existing GP. Only one home had experienced difficulties in registering with a GP and complained that the service received was consistently poor. However, we observed little involvement of health services in terms of preventive work. This is a matter of some concern given the potential health risks of this group of young people, including the disproportionate number of young women who become pregnant before leaving public care (Biehal *et al.* 1992; Garnett 1992).

The health issues for disabled children living in the two homes offering short-term breaks were rather different. Many of these young people suffered from severe, and occasionally terminal, conditions and required considerable attention from a range of health specialists. Co-ordination of health services could therefore be very complicated. Staff worked closely with parents in order to keep abreast of each child's needs. Sometimes they would attend meetings with parents to support them when a difficult decision had to be made regarding a child's health care, such as major surgery. Staff were also much more involved in themselves delivering health care, including administering complex medication, dealing with fits and convulsions, and providing physiotherapy. This was outlined in detailed care plans, often drawn up by consultant paediatricians. Sometimes international experts had been consulted in unusual cases. The seniority and expertise involved in assessment and diagnosis for this group stood in marked contrast to the much more inexpert approach to the problems of children in our sample without disabilities. This is not necessarily typical of the field (Audit Commission 1994; Department of Health Social Services Inspectorate 1994b), but in our study it was noticeably different from the other ten homes.

Indeed, we were astonished by the lack of involvement of virtually any other therapeutic service for non-disabled children. It seemed that, in view of the emotional and behavioural difficulties the majority of children living in these homes had experienced and presented, some at least would benefit from some form of counselling, group work or other expert therapeutic help. Yet this was extremely rare. One private home was particularly impressive and provided children with access to play and art therapy as well as providing counselling services for parents. Two homes in South were also making increasing use of child guidance services, which both were finding valuable; and in one home for younger children some counselling was available. Generally, however, there seemed little consistency in the nature and extent of such provision and it was often totally absent.

Education

The education of children in care has been a matter traditionally neglected by researchers (Jackson 1987). In more recent years this has been remedied to some extent, largely as a result of findings indicating the low achievements of this group of children. In school, children in care perform poorly in relation to their peers (Department of Health Social Services Inspectorate and Office for Standards in Education 1995; Fletcher-Campbell and Hall 1990; Heath, Colton and Aldgate 1994; Osborn and St Clair 1987), and studies of care leavers have shown that the majority of young people leave care with no educational qualifications (Biehal *et al.* op. cit.; Cheung and Heath 1994). These problems have been exacerbated by an increase in the numbers of young people looked after who are non-attenders or excluded from school (Brodie 1995; Brodie and Berridge 1996; Stirling 1992). This has potentially serious consequences, including unemployment and involvement in criminal activity (Devlin 1996; Graham and Bowling 1995).

While many of the educational difficulties experienced by children in residential care are related to earlier disadvantage, it has been argued that social work processes have failed to enhance the educational opportunities of this group (Fletcher-Campbell and Hall 1990). Changes of placement and the fact that education may have been given a low priority by social workers are among the issues which, it is suggested, need to be addressed. Within children's homes it has been noted that there is often a lack of educational stimulus and that residential staff fail to give sufficient attention to schooling, for example regarding homework (Berridge *et al.* 1997).

During our preliminary visits to homes staff often said that, following behavioural management, education was the second greatest general problem. In view of the seriousness of the issue, therefore, particular attention was given to schooling within our observations. Attention was focused on three main issues: the educational environment of the home; the nature of links between children's homes and schools; and the way in which issues of non-attendance and exclusion were dealt with by residential staff.

Educational environment

Existing research into the educational environment of children's homes has
suggested that units lack books and other educational materials and are somewhat
dull places in which to live (Berridge 1985; Berridge *et al.* 1997; Jackson 1989).
This was certainly true of the majority of the adolescent homes we visited. Even
where the decoration and furnishings were pleasant, there was often very little to
do. We consistently recorded an absence of books and magazines. In three homes
we found copies of the excellent *Who Cares?* magazine for children in care, but
these frequently lay in the office. In one home staff refused to give it to the young
people on the grounds that 'they would only rip it up'. One 17-year-old girl said
to the researcher, in a moment of particular boredom: 'You know what I'd really
love right now? A colouring book'. In this respect homes for younger children,
one short breaks home and some private homes performed distinctly better and
we found a reasonable number of attractive up-to-date books as well as an
assortment of educational games. However, few materials relating to minority
ethnic groups were available, with the exception of the Borough home where
black images and minority cultures were more in evidence. Staff also read bedtime
stories to younger children. In one private home a ten-year-old was keen to show
the researcher his drawing of a scene from *Charlie and the Chocolate Factory* and
talked enthusiastically with his keyworker about the chapter they were due to
read that night.

Only two homes, one in South and one private home, received a daily
newspaper. It was noticeable, however, that when researchers bought newspapers
and left these around a home, they were read by young people and interest was
expressed in various news items. Television news broadcasts were equally rarely
watched, all of which added to the sense of 'social disconnectedness' raised earlier.
This seemed to represent another form of institutionalisation, perhaps made more
insidious by virtue of its unconscious nature.

Somewhat to our surprise, television was watched quite rarely in the majority
of the homes. Indeed, children often seemed to have little enthusiasm for the
medium and viewing was more often directed by the preferences of staff than
young people. Videos were rather more popular, with Disney films favourites for
both adolescents and younger children. In one adolescent home this led to the
rather bizarre evening programme of *Silence of the Lambs* followed by *Snow White*,
symbolising perhaps the contradictory characteristics and unmet needs of these
adolescents. Seldom was television used strategically, for example to help
promote adult–child interaction, calm children before bedtime or to diffuse a
tense situation. There was also little encouragement to watch programmes of
educational value.

Overall, however, staff tried to encourage young people who were attending
school and, for example, children were usually asked how they had enjoyed their

day. Homework was also usually checked and staff tried to be sensitive to the situation of young people who were irregular attenders. In some cases strenuous efforts were made to encourage attendance – on one occasion bribery, in the form of a new pair of boots, was exercised. Yet many opportunities to enhance children's education were lost and practice frequently varied among staff. As has already been noted, facilities for homework were sometimes unsatisfactory. The fact that the majority of children had their own bedrooms meant that young people usually had a quiet space; on the other hand, tables on which to work were more often to be found in communal areas.

We were pleased to discover that children in the majority of our 12 homes had the opportunity to go on a range of trips and activities. Many homes, despite tight budgets, also tried hard to ensure children had an annual holiday. Destinations varied from Butlins to a trip to France. Many children had never before seen the seaside. A few children, mainly in the younger age group, had participated in school trips abroad. Disabled children were also involved in a wide variety of such activities, despite the difficulties regarding organisation and transport. In one home staff were pleased that their managerial transfer to children's services, and consequently the narrowing of their age group, meant that outside events could be more focused – it had previously been difficult to accommodate both adults' and children's preferences.

Liaison with schools

Links with schools were variable but were generally better than managers' accounts of relationships between social services and education. Staff often agreed that some schools would 'bend over backwards' to help a young person remain in school, while others were perceived as being only too willing to 'kick them out'. In some of the homes we visited, staff were on first name terms with teachers and were appreciative of positive links. This was more true in North than in South, largely as a result of the variation in the numbers of young people attending school. Even where there were disagreements over practice, however, it was widely recognised that schools faced a difficult task when dealing with these young people. Many staff expressed considerable sympathy for teachers dealing alone with a child with behavioural difficulties in a class of 35 or more: it was difficult enough for three residential workers with only six. Staff were aware of few links with other education services, such as educational psychology or educational welfare, and it seemed that older pupils were unlikely to receive this specialist help if social services had taken a prominent role (Roaf and Lloyd 1995). This strikes us as both illogical and regrettable.

The situation tended to be rather more positive for younger children, where staff reported various examples of situations where teachers had made major efforts to maintain a child in school. In one home – this was the only example –

residential staff had helped out as classroom assistants and felt that this had improved their understanding of the problems children experienced and posed in both situations. Generally, too, there was a greater sense of urgency among staff working with younger children in dealing with any educational problems which emerged.

Private homes were rather different, as two of these operated their own educational units. Rather surprisingly, few if any links seemed to exist with mainstream education in the local education authority. One of the homes had successfully reintegrated one or two children but this was not common. Heads of homes complained that local schools were at best unco-operative and at worst hostile. The consequence of this was that young people had restricted access to wider peer networks and thus tended to be more isolated. Other educational support services were also more likely to be inaccessible, though one home employed its own educational psychologist on a contract basis.

Attendance and exclusion

The issue of school exclusion has achieved considerable prominence in recent years, mainly as a result of the dramatic increase in the numbers of permanent exclusions taking place (Brodie and Berridge 1996; Department for Education and Employment 1993; Hayden *et al.* 1996). The majority of exclusions take place at secondary school level, specifically Years 10 and 11 (age 14–16 years), but an increase in the number of primary school pupils being excluded has also been observed (Hayden *et al.* 1996.). Certain groups have been identified as especially vulnerable to being excluded, including children with special educational needs and those looked after by local authorities. Gender and ethnicity are significant factors: boys are at least four times more at risk of exclusion than girls and African-Caribbean males (and to a lesser extent females) have been shown to be at particular risk (Brodie 1995; Brodie and Berridge 1996; Gillborn and Gipps 1996).

Considerable ambiguity surrounded the day-to-day experience of children who were excluded or were non-attenders. The majority of non-attenders lived in adolescent homes but one child of primary school age was also excluded on a fixed-term basis during our visit. In most homes exclusion appeared to be viewed as an inevitable part of life in a children's home and little action seemed to be taken. It was sometimes remarked that homes went through 'phases' when a high proportion of children were attending. However, no attempts had been made to identify factors which might help prevent a downturn or, alternatively, to produce the conditions necessary for high attendance. More often, problems were attributed to group dynamics and the view that the non-attendance of one child would encourage others not to attend. Staff also tended to be poorly informed regarding exclusion, often being unclear as to a child's precise educational status.

The term 'exclusion' was therefore used erroneously to cover a variety of types of non-attendance. This corresponds with research suggesting that a high proportion of the 'looked after' group are excluded on an 'informal' basis, without recourse to official procedures (Brodie 1995; Brodie and Berridge 1996; Stirling 1992). Unfortunately, the lack of information which staff possessed about schooling generally and exclusion specifically meant that they were ill-equipped to challenge exclusions effectively. On one occasion, having been requested, the researcher provided details about how an appeal might be made. Staff were grateful for this information and the issue was followed up with positive results. But the lack of such information meant that the education of many young people was effectively being left to chance and individual initiative, and this situation is clearly unsatisfactory.

As has already been described, children who were not attending school did little during the day. Staff recognised that this situation was undesirable but were typically unsure how they should respond. Many commented that they were not teachers and could not be expected to fulfil this role. It was argued that to provide any sort of education, however informal, would permit the education department to evade its responsibilities to these young people. Staff therefore felt 'dumped on', as they often put it, and were sometimes angry that schools refused to set schoolwork following an exclusion. However, staff also felt uneasy about allowing children to drift throughout the day and were conscious that this could lead them into trouble. In addition to this, there was uncertainty as to how children who were excluded should be treated. Staff were anxious to convey to the rest of the group that non-attendance was undesirable, and often tried to demonstrate this by refusing to allow children to watch television throughout the day and by insisting that children arose at a reasonable time.

Children excluded from school generally had access to some home tuition, though this was usually limited to approximately three hours each week. Staff in North were much less clear than those in South regarding home tuition arrangements, while workers in private homes were vaguer still about children's entitlements in this respect. During our fieldwork visits we encountered only one home tutor; although it was noted that there are issues about where home tuition should take place, it was generally felt that the children's home itself was an inappropriate location. However, the overriding view was that the amount of provision was wholly inadequate.

There is little doubt that staff were placed in a difficult situation by the numbers of young people not attending school. These difficulties were compounded by the lack of clear policy on the issue, either at the level of the home or the local authority. Inconsistency in practice was the inevitable result. Whether a child was expected to read or study, for example, often depended on the member of staff on duty or how busy a shift happened to be. This was well illustrated during one visit when a child was kept occupied with various activities during one day, then given nothing to do the next. At a core group meeting for a recent arrival in another home, education was high on the agenda and the head of home consistently made the point that the young person could not stay at the home without an educational placement. This information lacked credibility for the young person: it was well known to everyone at the meeting that none of the young people currently in the home were attending school. It was also instructive for the researcher to hear mutterings over the breakfast table as the children resident in this home advised an emergency admission that, 'if you live here you don't really have to go to school. Just stay at home!'.

It was noticeable, however, that when even a degree of structure was introduced to the daily life of a home, children were anxious to adhere to this. This was evident in one private home which provided education on site. The resident group here had experienced highly disrupted educational careers, usually involving a series of exclusions. During the researcher's visit the teacher was absent but the young people without exception requested staff for some alternative activity and were clearly at a loss about what to do without school.

While the picture regarding education was undeniably gloomy, some positive practice did filter through. Although exclusions sometimes occurred among the younger children, staff tended to take a more proactive stance; exclusions were more likely to be anticipated and preventive action taken. One home (G) benefited from the strenuous efforts of an education co-ordinator. Greater emphasis was also put on maintaining some sort of school structure to the day, even to the extent of wearing school uniform during school hours.

However, the contrast in the educational experience of children in the different categories of home was most marked in relation to children with severe learning disabilities. Without exception all the children in the two homes visited attended (special) school. This was particularly significant in view of the serious health and behavioural problems of many of these young people (see Chapter 4). Staff in these homes found it difficult to conceive of exclusion as a possibility, far less a problem. The attitudes of schools to the behaviour of this group of young people was also different. During a visit to a school attended by young people from the short breaks home in North, it was clear that the head teacher and staff did not regard exclusion as an option. This adds to the interesting comparisons we have noted in this study between services for children with disabilities and those without.

Conclusion

Having broadly outlined patterns of daily life in the 12 children's homes, let us now contrast this with the situation depicted in 1985. Comparing qualitative data is much more complex than presenting comparative statistics. It has been facilitated by intentionally adopting a common structure to the research (apart from the addition of the short breaks category), and having one researcher involved in both studies is also an advantage. Yet memories can be unreliable, certainly in this case, and it has been useful to have the second researcher scrutinise what was actually written in 1985.

In terms of physical environment, children's homes in these three local authorities have improved over the decade. They are now smaller, more intimate and their external appearance is less institutional. Homes are mostly in the midst of communities, which residents generally prefer; although, as we have noted, this also has disadvantages. It should not be overlooked that these considerations would not apply to young people from Borough, who could be placed in private homes many miles from London. Internally, most homes are better decorated, maintained and equipped than they were. Young people seldom have to share rooms. In contrast to these comforts, neighbours' and public attitudes towards children's homes and their residents have hardened. In a decade in which economic turbulence has had a serious impact on children and family life (Bradshaw 1990; Kumar 1993), and the extent of victimisation, including sexual abuse, experienced by the 'looked after' population is better understood, this growing intolerance is regrettable.

Improved physical conditions have been paralleled by a decline in traditional institutional practices such as in methods of transport, purchasing clothing and the buying and serving of food. Furnishings would not look out of place in an ordinary household. All of this is helped by the fact that most children's homes are now very small – half the size of the 1985 equivalents – although *in toto* probably no less bureaucratic. Other features, however, make these establishments less homely than their predecessors. No adults now live in – a major departure. Sibling groups are very rare in local authority homes and most residents stay for only a brief duration. These factors generate a feeling of impermanence and suggest that the main task is to provide shelter for the young. Another difference is that resident groupings are now more homogeneous. Many homes also have a clearer sense of their specific purpose. This helps in achieving objectives, as we shall see in Chapter 7, but it can make homes more unnatural.

Children's homes are noticeably better staffed than before. Though its practice is uneven, the overall quality of relationships between staff and residents has improved. A major advance, as we noted, concerns staff attitudes towards birth families and the maintenance of links. While not minimising the difficulties of parents and the problems they frequently caused, staff were nevertheless positive about the benefits of continuing contact and critical, undermining remarks were rare.

Notable differences existed among our 12 homes but a number of general improvements seem to have occurred over the decade in the residential child care sector. However, new problems have emerged, such as behavioural management, which is no doubt linked to some degree to the changing and more complex nature of the resident population. The inter-agency and multi-professional dimensions of the work, if anything, have also deteriorated. Relationships with field social workers ('care managers'), beset with differences in ideology and status, have not improved. With the exception of homes for younger children, foster care and its associated structures seemed largely irrelevant for the residents we encountered. It had often been tried and failed, and it was felt that caring for these young people would simply be beyond the capacity of available households. Consequently, relationships between most residential homes and fostering professionals were not strong.

However, a major contrast between this and the 1985 study lies in the field of education. School non-attendance barely features in the earlier report and the term 'school exclusion' was not once used. Instead, emphasis in 1985 was on issues such as schooling achievement and the potential disruption to education caused by changes in placements. Gaining access to schooling and ensuring attendance were not major problems. Of course, as we have argued, many of the current resident group a decade ago would have been receiving residential education rather than attending local day schools. Whatever other benefits a more community-oriented approach may have introduced, education has not been one of them. Changes in education legislation and policy have also discriminated against this group. Hence developments in social work policy and those in education have not been complementary. This applies at central government level but also within local authorities. It was unusual for coherent policies to be described to us between social services and education departments, although the current crisis may help bring this about.

Summary points

- The external appearance of the 12 homes was usually non-institutional. Internal decor and state of repair varied.

- Most of the 12 homes did not have Statements of Purpose – three years after the legislation required them. The position was better in North than in South. However, those Statements that did exist were often general and uninformative, as well as out of date.

- Relationships between young people and staff were usually informal, pleasant and friendly. Young people enjoyed being with staff and sought their company. Residents kept busy in the evenings, especially in homes for younger children and the short breaks facilities.

- With some exceptions, most homes had not thought particularly about how to meet the specific needs of girls, members of minority ethnic groups and care leavers.

- Behavioural control was a major issue in all homes and an area in which staff frequently lacked confidence. Particularly regarding adolescents, staff often seemed passive and preventive strategies were not developed. In many cases, young people acknowledged that they expected more control than they actually received and staff did not recognise the skills at their disposal. Interestingly, staff working with disabled children were less anxious about behaviour management, although their young people were no less challenging.

- Encouragingly, staff were positive about birth families and most residents maintained contact. However, parental visits to children's homes continue to be very rare.

- Children were usually active in their communities, although there was a strong sense of 'social disconnectedness' between most homes and their local environment. Neighbours were mostly hostile to the presence of a children's home. Apart from the benefits of community integration there were also disadvantages, including levels of local offending and the possible vulnerability of young women.

- Residential staff generally reported better relationships with outside agencies than with social workers. Interestingly, very positive links existed with the police.

- In contrast to the short breaks group, we were dismayed to find very few therapeutic services offered to children without disabilities.

- High quality learning resources were absent from most homes. However, staff generally encouraged young people attending school, asked if they had enjoyed their day and tried to ensure that homework was completed. Liaison with schools varied but was particularly positive in the case of short breaks homes and units accommodating younger children.

- A major problem was school non-attendance. Staff were often unclear about the exact status of non-attenders. Homes were also uncertain what pupils not attending school should do during the day: teachers provided little assistance in developing out of school programmes. Inter-agency policies at the level of the local authority and residential home were generally lacking.

- There was much variation in practices between homes. Yet in comparison with the 1985 research, improvements to children's homes over the decade include their external and internal appearance, size, level of staffing and quality of relationships. In contrast the inter-agency and multi-professional dimensions of the work have probably worsened. This includes relationships with social workers, colleagues in fostering services and education professionals.

6

Staffing

As we have shown, young people living in children's homes are frequently among the most damaged and disadvantaged in our society. However, surprisingly little is known about those who are employed to care for them. Few studies have focused specifically on residential child care staff (exceptions are Cawson 1978 and Millham *et al.* 1980). This imbalance has been addressed by the most recent group of studies on residential care, three of which give detailed attention to the culture and daily experience of staff working in children's homes, as well as to their qualifications and training (Brown *et al.* forthcoming; Sinclair and Gibbs 1996; Whitaker, Archer and Hicks 1996).

Residential work involves a wide variety of tasks and skills. We have seen that these can include providing support and reassurance; encouraging recreation or relaxation; offering personal, physical care to disabled children; placating a frustrated teacher; and dealing with disorder. Sinclair and Gibbs (1996) have sought to classify these tasks and show that residential staff are most involved in the following: keeping order and general supervision; showing concern for young people; social training; and acting as a keyworker. In carrying out these tasks liaison with other agencies is also necessary and staff are required to interact with a complex network of individuals external to the home (Whitaker 1996.).

One of the aims of our research was to find out about those who worked in the children's homes – their biographical characteristics and working experience but also their views on different aspects of residential life. As with the rest of the study, both quantitative and qualitative methods were used to capture these different dimensions of the staff world. A brief questionnaire was designed to collect biographical information including details of position, age, gender, ethnicity, experience and professional and educational qualifications. While we recognise the often important role of ancillary staff such as cooks and cleaners, we confined the questionnaire to those with specific child care responsibility. A hundred and three questionnaires of the potential 148 were returned, giving us a response rate of 70 per cent. Given the larger staff teams, we did not actually meet all employees, which made retrieving the questionnaires more difficult. Only 1 of the 12 homes (A) returned noticeably fewer questionnaires. Heads of homes were also asked for information on the number and organisation of staff working in their unit.

Understanding of the daily duties and experience of residential staff was largely obtained through our participant observation in the homes (see Chapter 5). Indeed, given the absence of young people of all ages during the day, we were probably more able to observe staff than children. We also tried to carry out semi-structured interviews with child care staff. This was not always easy – interviews were frequently interrupted by the telephone ringing or were carried out while helping wash the dishes from the evening meal. In some homes staff were so busy that we were obliged to collate information from general conversations to represent their views. While we do not consider that this necessarily renders the information less valid, account should be taken of the difficulties encountered while collecting these data and future researchers should bear this in mind. It should also be noted that while staff often found it difficult to find time to talk to us individually, the vast majority were keen to tell us about their views. Interviews frequently seemed to perform something of a therapeutic function in providing space within the sometimes stressful environment of the children's home for staff to talk freely about their experience of residential work.

An important dimension of our research with staff was also a lengthy semi-structured interview, usually lasting at least two hours, with the head of home. In addition to the areas covered in the staff interviews, we also asked questions about wider issues such as the referral process, management support, the role of residential care in the child care policy of the local authority and, where relevant, about the relationships between private homes and local authorities.

Each of these methods yielded a considerable amount of information on residential staff, which we have arranged thematically. We have also tried to focus on areas which heads of homes and residential staff identified as most significant. However, comparative information on the nature of the staff group is also important and the chapter begins by considering the characteristics and organisation of the staff working in the 12 homes. This includes the qualifications and training of the staff group, factors which have often been associated with their low status. We then examine the external structures within which each home is embedded, such as links with management and referral processes, which had important implications for the daily experience of residential staff. These had often changed many times since the 1985 study, but of greater interest in this chapter are staff perceptions of the changes which have taken place in the service delivered to young people. In our interviews with staff, two issues emerged as crucial. First, staff were concerned about the nature of the resident group and particularly the control problems which they felt had increased over the years. Second, matters related to status and morale continued to loom large for residential staff.

The staff group

The Children Act 1989 guidance points out that the number of staff in a home should depend on the role and purpose of the unit and that no fixed ratios can therefore be specified (Department of Health 1991b). It is clear, however, that there has been a substantial increase in the number of staff working in children's homes. The 1985 study found 136 full- and part-time child care staff in the 20 homes visited, an average (mean) of 7 staff in each home. In contrast, 148 staff worked in the 12 homes which form the present sample, with a corresponding average of 12 staff. We should not overlook the fact that the average children's home nowadays has half the number of residents compared with 1985. The York study found a similar overall level of 10 staff to each home.

The fact that the typical children's home now contains more staff than children reflects both changes in policy as well as concerning the resident group. Overall there were almost two staff to each resident. Adult:child ratios, therefore, are now similar in foster and residential care. Short breaks and adolescent homes were the most generously staffed (both 2.2:1), followed by private homes and units for younger children (both 1.6:1). Excluding disabled children and taking into account age differences, private homes in our sample each had about two fewer members of staff than local authority facilities catering for a similar number of children. Staffing ratios were higher in North than in South. One in six workers was part-time. A similar proportion of staff were temporary employees (18 per cent). This rose to almost a third in the adolescent homes and approximately a quarter in the short breaks and private facilities. Very few temporary staff were involved with younger children. There were noticeably more temporary employees in South than in North.

Female staff outnumbered males by six to four. The gender imbalance is slightly less than in 1985, when there were twice as many female residential workers, though larger homes tended to have more male staff. If we examine the gender balance in different categories of home, we find that in homes for adolescents and in private homes there was an almost even balance between male and female staff. This contrasted with the situation in homes for younger children, where there were almost twice as many females as males. In the two short breaks homes the imbalance was more noticeable still, with only 6 male staff from a group of 23. This may reflect concerns about abuse issues in regard to the younger age group and children with severe learning disabilities, although one should not assume that adolescents are immune from these problems.

The vast majority of the group – 90 per cent – were white. The remaining ten members of staff described themselves variously as African-Caribbean, African, Caribbean and African/White. The small number of staff from minority ethnic groups was concentrated in just two homes (I and L), both located in Borough. Heads of homes in other areas acknowledged problems in recruiting staff from minority ethnic groups. Overall, however, the ethnicity of the staff group broadly matched the sample of young people. The exceptions were homes J and K, both private homes which admitted children from minority ethnic groups but had been unsuccessful in recruiting black staff. Staff in these homes did not necessarily view this situation as problematic, arguing either that they were aware of cultural issues or that the young person did not perceive his or her ethnicity to be problematic. Yet, as we have noted, heads of homes were not always able to specify the ethnic background of these young people, and it did not appear that staff had received in-depth training on equal opportunity and anti-discriminatory issues.

Training and qualifications

The inferior status associated with residential social work has frequently been linked to lack of staff training and professional qualifications. Residential social work has often been perceived as intuitive, requiring emotional qualities such as sensitivity and compassion rather than specific qualifications. However, while these qualities are important, training can 'guide their most effective application' (Millham *et al.* 1980, p.1). Numerous official reports have called for an increase in the number of qualified residential staff. Scandals in residential care have also highlighted the issue. The Utting Report, in a survey of 20 local authorities, found that 70 per cent of child care staff and 20 per cent of officers-in-charge in local authority homes were professionally unqualified and described this situation as 'deplorable' (Department of Health 1991a). The report concluded that all heads of homes and a proportion of care staff, about one-third in all, should hold a social work qualification.

The difficulties associated with this position have been well rehearsed. Training is expensive and may remove staff from their place of work for lengthy periods of time. Many residential workers have used professional training mainly as a passport out of the sector. One person, returning from a course, can also have problems trying to implement her or his ideas in isolation. Moreover, it has proved difficult to identify a qualification which is appropriate to the work of residential social workers. Traditionally the residential component of social work qualifications has been insignificant, and the skills obtained through such a qualification may well seem irrelevant. Some social work trainers are also unsympathetic to residential care ideologically, so it may actually be counter-productive. Indeed Warwickshire, which closed all of its own residential homes in the late 1980s, maintained that one important step in its strategy had been to send away all its residential workers to be trained: they thus returned less committed to the sector (Cliffe with Berridge 1991). The Warner Report (Department of Health 1992), which built on the work of Utting, argued that a separate qualification for residential staff should be developed. Throughout the 1980s a number of new measures, such as the Department of Health's Residential

Child Care Initiative, sought to enhance training opportunities for residential social workers.

Table 6.1 reveals comparative professional qualifications in the current and previous research. On this occasion, 16 per cent of the sample as a whole were professionally qualified. A further 6 per cent had taken one of the two relevant Open University courses. Perhaps surprisingly, only three members of staff had completed a National Vocational Qualification (NVQ), suggesting that this had so far failed to make an impact. We were aware, however, that some other members of staff had begun NVQ courses or were planning to start. Therefore, as a proportion, twice as many residential staff were professionally qualified in 1995 compared with 1985, although this still applies to barely one in six overall.

Table 6.1 Professional qualifications of full-time staff, 1995 and 1985

	Heads of homes		Other staff		All staff	
	1995	1985	1995	1985	1995	1985
Diploma/Certificate in Social Work (DipSW/CQSW)	1	1	5	5	6 (6%)	6 (4%)
Certificate in Social Service	3	0	7	0	10 (10%)	0 (0%)
Certificate in the Residential Care of Children and Young People	0	1	0	3	0 (0%)	4 (3%)
Open University Courses K254/P653	1	0	5	0	6 (6%)	0 (0%)
NVQ	0	0	3	0	3 (3%)	0 (0%)
In-service training	4	13	34	35	38 (38%)	48 (35%)
None of the above	2	5	36	73	38 (38%)	78 (57%)
TOTAL	(n=11)	(n=20)	(n=90)	(n=116)	(n=101) (100%)	(n=136) (100%)

The extent of educational qualifications in our samples appears unchanged over the decade. Thirteen per cent of all staff in the current study were university graduates, which is similar to 1985. This is slightly higher than the educational achievements for the wider population, taking age structure into account, where some 11 per cent are graduates (Office of Population, Censuses and Surveys 1996, table 10.3). Interestingly, staff in private homes were better qualified educationally than their local authority colleagues, with the proportion of graduates being nearer a quarter.

If we examine heads of homes separately, in 1985 only 2 of the 20 had obtained social work qualifications, compared with 4 of the 11 now (home H was without a head at the time of our visit). Hence heads of homes were more likely to be professionally qualified than before, but this applied to only 1 in 3 of our sample. (Among the 11 deputy heads of homes, 3 were professionally qualified.)

The pattern of qualifications varied according to region, a finding which corresponds with other studies (Department of Health 1991a, 1992). The proportion of qualified staff was greater in North, where a third were qualified, compared with fewer than one in ten in South. In addition, in South the three group managers were each professionally qualified social workers. However, as they did not have a significant presence in homes during the time of our visits, we have excluded them from the above statistics. Only one professionally qualified member of staff was found in the private sector. Although we did not collect systematic data on this issue, the regional variation seemed to reflect different attitudes in the two local authorities towards the secondment of staff to qualifying training courses. This was still favoured in North, while South had adopted a strategy of increasing the amount of in-service training available to staff. Interestingly, this contrasts sharply with the geographical spread of qualifications found in 1985, when no child care staff in North, including heads of homes, had undertaken any social work qualifying training.

A quarter of staff returning questionnaires stated that they had undergone no relevant training whatsoever, including in-service courses. Again, the deficiency was most evident in private homes, affecting two in five workers. Staff in private homes when interviewed were much more likely than others to voice concerns over access to training and cited this as one of the main disadvantages of working in the independent sector. The proprietor of one private home informed us that the employment of untrained and unqualified staff was a deliberate policy, on the grounds that qualified staff had to be trained out of 'bad habits'. This statement is a dangerous one as similar sentiments have been expressed by senior staff who have developed abusive regimes (Berridge and Brodie 1996).

One noticeable change which had taken place was the amount of in-service training available to staff working for local authorities. This had not been anticipated at the beginning of the study and specific areas of training were not identified in advance, but overall 35 per cent of staff had received some form of in-service training (rising to over half of the staff group in South). Though the same proportion as in 1985, it was apparent this time round that the span of courses attended was much more extensive, ranging from instruction in control and restraint to courses on drugs awareness. A trend seemed to be developing whereby employers felt they obtained better value from in-service training rather than sending individuals away on lengthy secondments. No doubt there is a financial consideration. Apart from its influence on skills development, this trend also has important implications for professional status.

Residential experience

As Sinclair and Gibbs (1996) emphasise, it is important to set experience alongside the extent of professional qualifications. Utting (Department of Health 1991a) suggests that within the service, the picture is one of a core of residential care stalwarts surrounded by a wider group who have been in post for only a short time. Our sample revealed an impressive pool of experience (Figure 6.1). We questioned staff on two dimensions of experience: how long they had worked in residential care with young people and how long they had been in their current unit. Twenty-nine per cent of child care staff had worked with young people for more than five years, with a further 31 per cent for over ten years. Only 13 per cent of staff had worked with young people for under a year. The average level of experience has thus risen from three years in 1985 to nearer seven years a decade later. If we distinguish heads of homes we find a very experienced group. Nine of the 11 had more than 10 years' residential or social work experience with young

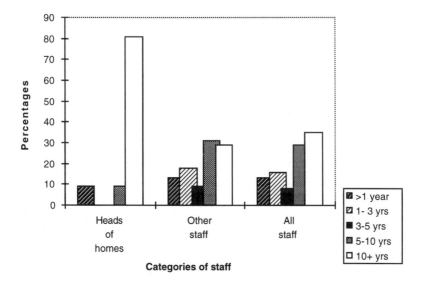

Figure 6.1 Experience of residential child care work

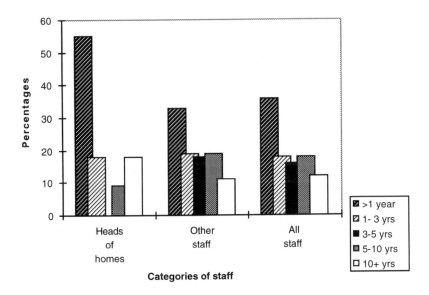

Figure 6.2 Time working in current residential home

people. Interestingly, the age structure of the staff group seems also to have changed since 1985, with an average age over 35 years now, compared with 30 in 1985.

However, the situation is very different if we examine the length of time staff had spent working in their *current* children's home (Figure 6.2). It was revealed in Chapter 2 that only 4 of the staff in the 20 homes in the 1985 study were still residential child care workers in the same agencies 10 years later. In the current study, over a third of current staff had worked in their establishment less than a year and over half, in total, less than three years. It is striking that many heads of homes were recent arrivals, with 6 of the 11 having joined within the previous 12 months. This stands in marked contrast to the situation in 1985, where the average time in post of heads of homes was five years rather than barely one year now.

It is notable that staff in North were a much more stable group than in other areas – approaching half had stayed in the same children's home for more than five years, compared with a third of staff in South. If we also look at the different categories of home, we find that staff in the short breaks homes, followed by staff working in homes for adolescents, had on average worked for a longer period in the same unit. These same two categories of staff also ranked highest in terms of their experience in working with young people.

Although we are dealing with a small sample, these findings seem to have important implications. First of all, we can reiterate the 1985 conclusion that any lingering perception of residential staff as an occupational group characterised by high turnover is misplaced: mobility is related more to place of work than residential work *per se*. This pattern can at least partially be attributed to the high degree of organisational change we found in each of the three local authorities. The best example of this is home I, the facility in Borough offering short-term care for disabled children. A core of the staff group had been transferred there following the closure of other residential homes in the borough. One member of staff had recently worked at *six* other children's homes in the authority, each of which had eventually closed. His arrival hardly inspired confidence in the staff group. The private homes in the sample had also recently recruited a high proportion of their current staff groups. As we shall see, the stability of the staff group will emerge as important in our discussion of the quality of care offered in our sample of children's homes.

Staffing structures

The effectiveness of a staff team is influenced to a considerable degree by its organisation and management. The staffing structures of the 12 homes varied, both regionally and across categories of home. Furthermore, 'reorganisation' or 'restructuring' was a common experience for all the homes in the sample and was perceived to have had a major impact on the experience of staff working within the units. Our York colleagues have shown that frequent reorganisation can jeopardise the quality of care delivered (Sinclair and Gibbs 1996).

North had retained a fairly traditional structure in its establishments, with a head of home and deputy. Temporary staff were rarely used: those we did encounter had often been working in the same home for as long as some permanent staff. As we saw, staff groups in North were more stable than in South. The homes also benefited from their close geographical proximity, which contributed to the development of good relationships between staff working in different units.

The most innovative, if probably the least successful, form of staffing structure was to be found in South, where the traditionally central role of the head of home had been all but abolished (see Chapter 3). Instead a system of 'group management' had been introduced. This involved a 'group manager' being responsible for two or three residential units. 'Assistant managers' were in charge of the day-to-day running of the homes but also worked between two or more homes. The result was a high degree of confusion, mainly resulting from the lack of clarity surrounding management roles and responsibilities.

The role of group manager was especially ambiguous. Their work appeared to be more related to policy development than the detailed functioning of the children's home, yet they remained nominally 'in charge'. During our visits they emerged as somewhat shadowy figures, flitting occasionally into the home *en route* to a meeting. Their inaccessibility is demonstrated by the fact that each of our 'head of home' interviews in these circumstances was in fact carried out with assistant managers. Yet assistant managers were also frequently absent and each home in South was effectively without an officer-in-charge for substantial periods of time. The unsatisfactory nature of the situation was exacerbated by the fact that the homes in South were widely spread geographically, thus limiting further the amount of time a manager could spend at each.

In order to facilitate the internal running of the homes, the grade of senior residential worker had been fortified and these members of staff had been renamed 'shift leaders'. However, they lacked the authority to make many decisions and their role by no means compensated for the lack of leadership within the home. For example, when the researcher's wallet was stolen in home D, the shift leader consulted the assistant manager, who spoke to the group manager. By the time communication had been handed back down, the researcher had left the home and no one had confronted the residents in what was by now four days after the incident occurring. Young people subsequently admitted they were incredulous at the lack of response. South also made considerable use of temporary or 'Care Bank' staff and this further increased the instability of the staff group. Overall, the system lacked coherence. Residential staff found the situation unsatisfactory and where morale was perceived to be low this was sometimes linked to changes in the management system. Only one assistant manager felt that the system had been successful in achieving its aim of greater flexibility.

The situation in private homes differed again. Arrangements in each of the three homes were highly individualistic. In home K the manager exercised an exceptionally high degree of control, taking responsibility for liaison with other professionals and, with an administrative manager, most of the paperwork. Residential social workers were largely confined to child care tasks, and the close supervision of the resident group figured highly in their work. The proprietor, meanwhile (a different person to the manager), worked as a residential worker within the home, while retaining considerable influence over policy. This structure can largely be attributed to the small size of the home, which permitted a tight management system. In the two other private facilities, the units visited were part of a wider structure and staffing arrangements reflected this. In home L the system rather resembled the 'group management' in place in South, with one individual responsible for three units. However, the fact that these properties were situated side by side in the same street reduced the difficulties encountered in South. A senior residential worker was responsible for day-to-day activities, including for example the induction of new staff, and reference was also frequently made to the overall service manager. In home J, the head of the home was essentially in charge of the running of the unit, but the proprietor was also in frequent contact.

Management structures and support

As Chapter 3 demonstrated, each of the three local authorities was described by managers as having introduced a 'purchaser–provider' arrangement in services, though the exact implementation of this varied. Heads of homes were cautious in their judgement, feeling that the structure was insufficiently established to make firm conclusions. However, where opinions were voiced, the purchaser–provider split tended to be viewed negatively. An important criticism of this model in children's services has been that the care decisions of purchasing fieldworkers have suffered as a result of their increased isolation from colleagues involved in the daily care of children (Jones and Bilton 1994, p.39). Heads of homes in both North and South supported this concern, arguing that the greater fragmentation of the system had widened the gulf between fieldworkers and children's homes. Not only was there a greater sense of professionals being in a 'them and us' relationship, but the new care management system also distanced fieldworkers from young people. Although they had ultimate decision-making responsibility, it was argued that fieldworkers infrequently carried out direct work with young people and therefore knew them insufficiently.

As suggested in Chapter 3, heads of homes in all three areas we visited confirmed that recent changes in external management had been unhelpful, leaving them with less management support overall. In South the fact that management posts had been changed at the same time as staffing structures had led to an unstable situation; one assistant manager commented that, 'the roof has been put on the house without the foundations being laid'. It was also widely felt that managers had little direct experience of residential care and were, therefore, unable to appreciate the impact of the changes being made. Nevertheless, specific managers in both North and South were identified as being supportive, as well as the line-manager of the short breaks home in Borough.

Staff in local authority homes typically expressed scepticism towards external management, feeling that agencies had become increasingly business-oriented. Consequently they felt there was little real understanding of residential care. Inevitably communication was also sometimes raised as an issue, with complaints that management failed to take staff views into account, even where the decision would directly affect the residential unit. Such concerns were especially acute where a home was due to change premises, as was the case for three homes in North. In the Borough home offering short-term breaks (I), some staff were convinced that the facility would be privatised or would become more firmly embedded within adult services.

Generally, then, external management was perceived to make only a limited contribution to the running of the local authority homes we visited. However, heads of homes rated management as the most important group in terms of the introduction and development of policy in each facility. The head of home has become less influential in this respect compared with the previous study. Policy would be discussed with staff but their influence was considered to be fairly limited, except in the two short breaks homes where staff had been more actively involved. Interestingly, only the heads of the two homes for younger children included the views of young people as potentially significant in formulating policy within the home.

The situation tended to be rather different in private homes. Staff were more likely to express positive views towards their proprietors and managers. This seemed to result from the greater degree of managerial involvement in the everyday running of the homes and consequently better communication. In one home a residential worker remarked that while she had no illusions regarding the ambitions of the proprietors – 'they want to be another Barnardo's' – she appreciated the fact that she knew profits were being ploughed back into the units. The more direct management style was illustrated by the fact that heads of private homes tended to feel that policy development for the home was carried out in partnership with staff, though interestingly there was less awareness of wider legislative frameworks.

Referral and admission processes

One important indicator of the relationship between heads of homes and external management relates to the admission of young people to the units. As we have already shown, homes varied in the extent to which they had a clearly specified purpose. Even where heads of homes were able to describe the role of the home, however, they were sometimes unable to hold to their objectives due to their limited control over admission processes.

Chapter 4 has described the nature of the population of the 12 homes and it is clear that the majority were dealing with a more difficult population than previously. Heads of homes and staff alike agreed that they were now admitting the 'extreme end' of cases and that residents were more disturbed behaviourally and emotionally. Heads of the two homes for younger children also highlighted the greater incidence or awareness of sexual abuse. In view of the highly problematic group entering residential care, it is important to question whether an individual children's home represents the optimum placement for a young person.

It should also be considered whether individuals find themselves living with an appropriate group of young people. Indeed, there are some whose previous histories suggest that their entry into a group will endanger others. Thus it is necessary for heads of homes and staff to feel their views on admissions are being listened to; where there is a sense of lack of control over admissions this can add considerably to an already stressful job (Whitaker, Archer and Hicks 1996).

Referral processes varied according to the category of home and also by area. In South there was a conflict between the ideal, planned process of admission and the reality of emergency placements following a phone call from a fieldworker. This was a problem for all three homes. A panel system existed where specific cases were intended to be discussed among group managers. This could then be followed up by discussions with the staff group in the selected home. However, it was argued by heads of homes that only a core of fieldworkers actually used this system and ultimately, 'it boils down to whoever has an empty bed'. Recently the system had come under increasing pressure due to an embargo on out-of-county placements. This situation was clearly unsatisfactory and during our visits to the homes in South we observed more than once the pressure placed on the home when a fieldworker phoned requesting an emergency admission. In home D, which had experienced a number of problems in the months prior to our visit, the assistant manager felt the tide had turned and they were now being permitted to be more selective. However, the breathing space given to home D meant that other establishments came under greater pressure.

In North the filtering process was different and was instead related to the more specialised functions of the homes. Adolescents were initially placed in home A, which functioned as a short-term emergency unit. If child and family problems were not resolved, a subsequent placement was arranged. The majority of the adolescents we encountered in North had experienced at least one placement in home A. The greater specialisation of the units appeared to permit heads of homes to exercise greater control over admissions. The referral process for younger children was different again; the head of home received the initial referral and then met with the child's social worker. A senior member of staff also attended a review meeting prior to the admission. This seemed to work very well – the head of home felt able to maintain the home's objectives and the vast majority of admissions were planned.

In all three private homes, in contrast, there was a manager with responsibility for dealing with referrals and the associated negotiations with the local authority. In one, home referrals came mainly through 'Care Base' (a national database). In home K, which was some distance from the local authorities served, the manager was determined to avoid a situation where social workers simply sought to, 'get rid of a young person 100 miles away'. Unless a young person had seen and liked the home, they would not be admitted. Following admission, there was a trial period during which weekly meetings were held with the social worker. This home also refused to admit young people remanded by courts to the local authority or with a long history of arson. In homes J and L, a provisional decision to admit was made by the referrals officer, then discussed with the head of home. In these homes, which were part of a more complex organisational structure than home K, it was clear that the views of the head of home and also the staff group were taken into account when the decision was taken to admit a young person. Unsurprisingly, then, it seemed that the private sector exercised more stringent control over the referral process. It was both important and encouraging to find that the three private homes were not freely admitting all and sundry in an effort to fill empty beds or make money, although two of the homes had previously been more flexible in this while they were in the process of becoming established.

Most heads of homes interviewed were able to identify at least one child within their current group who had been inappropriately placed from the outset. There were several reasons for this. For private homes the groups they catered for were dependent on the types of referral they received. The head of home K stated that he was frequently under pressure from local authorities for their young people to be moved on prematurely. He also cited instances where he had requested the young person be moved because the local authority had refused to pay for the extra support which the home felt necessary. Such options are not available to most local authority homes. Encouragingly, the heads of the two other private homes were not subjected to pressures to move young people inappropriately.

Developments in residential child care

Our attempt to obtain the views of staff on the ways in which residential care had changed over recent years was of course influenced by the fact that some had not worked for long in the sector. Nonetheless, staff tended to find it easier to identify areas of deterioration than improvement and we were frequently regaled with a catalogue of complaints. As the discussion below demonstrates, these usually focused on young people themselves and specifically on increased levels of aggression and delinquency. Some residential staff, perhaps too romantically, compared this with an age when young people 'came in from school and put on their slippers', as one put it. Conditions of work were also criticised, including the amount of administration and, for some staff, the environment of the homes in which they were working. Fortunately, however, most staff were also able to discern some improvements in the service being offered. There tended to be relatively little consistency in responses about these, but comments included the fact that their standing with fieldworkers and other agencies was often better and that pay for residential staff had improved.

Young people

While examination of the care histories of young people enabled us to contrast the resident group with that found in 1985, we also tried to gauge staff perceptions of these changes. The earlier study identified four groups of young people: emergency admissions; young people awaiting foster placements, many of whom had already experienced fostering breakdowns; adolescents who maintained strong parental loyalties and rejected fostering; and those, usually adolescents, who had been in care for many years and for whom virtually everything else had been tried. Heads of homes were specifically asked whether these groups still existed and if they could identify any others. As short-term breaks for disabled children had not been examined as part of the 1985 study, the question was omitted in these two homes. Staff were also asked, but more generally, whether they could discern any changes in the circumstances and problems of young people entering the homes.

Responses largely depended on the experience of staff and heads of homes and also whether their work had been focused on any one group of young people. Most heads of homes agreed that all four groups still existed, though the head of one adolescent home thought that the final group of adolescents, those who had been in care for many years and for whom everything else had been tried, was less evident. The manager of one private home, on the other hand, argued that this group was the most prominent. Some variations on the typology were also suggested. Heads of homes felt that the young people referred were now more emotionally and behaviourally disturbed and the heads of the two homes for younger children also noted that sexual abuse was much more of a factor. School exclusion had resulted in a new set of problems, mainly for adolescents. Reference was also made to growing social problems more generally, such as poverty and unemployment.

In arguing that young people entering residential care had become a more difficult group, reference was frequently made to the control problems which resulted from trying to manage their behaviour. For some heads of homes behavioural control was the biggest problem they faced in their work. The issue was, if anything, emphasised even more strongly by residential staff. This is consistent with other research findings. Sinclair and Gibbs (1996) found that the areas which caused residential staff greatest concern were the progress made by residents and 'keeping order'. The key stresses in residential work identified by Whitaker *et al.* (1996) included the sense of powerlessness which staff experienced regarding young people's behaviour, particularly where they were felt to be misplaced or there was an inappropriate mix of residents. Our interviews revealed that, as with morale, the extent to which control was perceived as a problem sometimes varied considerably within the staff group. In some units which were currently experiencing few control problems, this was usually related to the nature of the resident group, and many staff felt that problems tended to occur in phases rather than being intrinsic to the home.

In two of the private homes, most staff seemed to have absorbed the philosophies on which their homes were based. In home K, where considerable emphasis was placed on the supervision of young people, all the members of staff interviewed commented that significant behavioural problems could be averted if appropriate supervision were in place. Similarly, in home L, it was argued that control issues could only be dealt with adequately through broader therapeutic work. This suggests that where staff are conscious of strategies through which behavioural problems can be tackled, they are less likely to perceive these difficulties as being overwhelming. We return to this issue in our next two chapters. It is also notable that staff in the two short breaks homes defined control issues quite differently. It was pointed out that while behavioural problems inevitably arose, staff benefited from advice from psychologists and other professionals. Again staff were clear about how they might begin to address the behaviour and stressed the need to create consistent practices with parents. Staff in other homes emphasised the importance of having positive relationships with young people, which reduced the need to use more extreme methods of control such as restraint. Reference was also made to the importance of a good staff team in preventing disorder.

In their attempts to explain serious behavioural problems, staff often referred to the issue of children's rights and children 'knowing too much'. It was felt that children had been empowered at the expense of staff, and that staff were consequently unable to deal effectively with behavioural issues. One member of staff expressed the views of many in saying, 'we're expected to deal with the most difficult young people in society yet we're not given the tools to do it with'. At the same time, some staff expressed the view that the fact that children had 'more voice' was a positive development. Such opinions appear contradictory but frequently emerged within the same interview. The fear that 'we have gone too far in thinking that young people can dictate the rules' also featured in the interview with the head of one private home. Concern about children's rights appeared to be linked to a strong sense that staff would not be supported by management should any untoward incident occur. Instances were cited where a staff member had restrained a young person and had then been disciplined. There is clearly a great deal of concern and confusion among residential staff on this issue which, as we saw in the previous chapter, often prevents more positive work from being achieved or even attempted.

Delinquency was perceived to be a problem in all the local authority homes for adolescents and in one home for younger children. Abuse of drugs and solvents, theft and some car crime were the main issues. These problems could be exacerbated when young people were remanded by the courts to local authority accommodation. This topic aroused strong feelings and it was almost unanimously agreed that such referrals to children's homes were inappropriate. The problems associated with 'remands' included their influence on the remainder of the resident group and their lack of commitment to living in the home. In North this was no longer happening as remands were being diverted effectively to youth justice, but many staff members had negative memories of the experience – one commented, 'we needed a bouncer and a nurse on the door'. In South, homes were still being referred remands and staff felt that this severely impaired the work they could undertake.

Status

Unlike some European countries (Madge 1994), staff in children's homes in Britain have long been viewed as having inferior status to their fieldwork colleagues. If social work generally has struggled to achieve status as a profession, residential social work has languished still further as the 'Cinderella to field social work' (Kahan 1994, p.255). This is linked to a variety of factors, including the equation of care-related work with women and the lack of professional qualifications among residential staff. This historical legacy is difficult to dislodge. However, while the public image of residential child care continues to be dogged by scandal, the sector has also been the focus of significant attention from government, which at long last has helped improve the overall status of residential staff (Berridge and Brodie 1996). The managers of two homes noted that the shift in language from 'houseparent' to 'residential social worker' symbolised the improved status which they felt had been one of the key changes of the past decade.

However, while there was a general sense among staff that status had improved, the picture was by no means entirely positive. Heads of homes and residential social workers almost overwhelmingly felt that they continued to have lower status in relation to their fieldwork colleagues, though this had improved somewhat. Frequent references were made to the view that they were perceived as 'baby-sitters' or, memorably, 'social workers in slippers'. Staff complained that their views were sometimes ignored, despite the fact that they often had better day-to-day knowledge of a young person. There was also a sense that children's homes tended to be viewed as a 'last resort' or a 'dumping ground' for young people and that the work carried out there was unappreciated. Nevertheless, it was acknowledged that there were considerable variations in relationships with fieldworkers and many residential staff cited instances where positive joint working had taken place. Residential social workers appreciated fieldwork where they could see an active commitment to the young person and where there was good communication with the children's home.

In addition to examining the status of residential work in comparison with social work more generally, we also asked staff about status in the local community. Residential staff in all areas were agreed that perceptions were usually negative. Heads of homes were also unanimous on this point. This was sometimes related to the scandal which has dogged the residential sector – one worker commented that there had been so much bad publicity he was embarrassed to tell anyone that he worked in a children's home. But it was also widely felt that the general public had little, if any, understanding of the work which took place in children's homes, and that perceptions of the young people who lived there were often distorted: 'We are the first port of call if anything goes wrong in the neighbourhood', remarked a head of home for younger children. Staff typically felt that such stereotypes about the resident group were unjustified and most felt that children looked after in residential care were still stigmatised. In some cases individual homes had also been damaged by negative publicity in the local media. This contrasted with the situation in the two short breaks homes, where staff felt their work had high status and was valued by members of the community.

Staff morale

There is little doubt that working in a residential unit is a highly stressful occupation. Merely visiting for less than a week was physically and emotionally exhausting. Not only are staff working directly with an extremely damaged group of young people, but patterns of work, such as long shifts, working unsocial hours and disturbed sleep, may contribute to low morale in a staff group. The traditional low status of residential work is also unhelpful. At the same time, however, significant rewards can be found – Whitaker *et al.* (1996) suggest that these include developing the ability to deal with difficult situations, seeing young people benefit from care and being a member of a supportive staff team.

Morale is a complex concept. Sinclair and Gibbs (1996) equated morale with 'job satisfaction' and asked individual staff to rate this on a four-point scale. Our approach took a rather different form and focused on morale across the staff group. Initially, staff when interviewed were asked in an open-ended question how they would assess morale in the home – no further guidance was provided. However, we also developed our own perception of staff morale during our periods of participant observation. In this we were guided by evidence of, for example, disposition, enthusiasm, the expression of positive and negative attitudes, and staff rivalry and conflict. The assessment of morale among staff in the 12 homes was inevitably affected by the timing of our visits. Occasionally these coincided with serious or even tragic events within a home and, understandably, morale in these units was lower than it might have been a few days before or after. However, there is an extent to which morale exists independently of such crises and it could be argued that dealing with these matters is a regrettable but inevitable part of working in a residential unit.

Certainly we did not find morale to be necessarily related to the current circumstances of the home. Morale was sometimes high, for example among staff working in homes where there was likely to be a change of premises, or where it was acknowledged that the resident group presented a considerable challenge. Staff in homes where morale was high, therefore, seemed more able to distinguish discrete problems – such as the behaviour of a particular child or the location of the unit – from their assessment of the overall situation within the home. One residential social worker, while commenting on the general feeling of insecurity which existed in the unit, at the same time remarked that his fellow staff members were 'a great bunch of people' and were usually doing the job for the right reasons. This suggests that, first of all, morale cannot be explained in terms of any single dimension of work in a home; and, second, that factors associated with low morale may be counterbalanced or become quite insignificant where other positive factors are in place.

Thus, as we have seen several times previously in this report, practices and experiences varied noticeably between our 12 homes. Generally we found morale to be higher in North than in South. Staff teams in North also worked better together, with less gossiping between shifts. In South, staff were more cynical about their work and saw fewer prospects for improvement. Home E, however, was the only unit where the extremely low level of morale was a matter of major concern, with staff continually using such terms as 'chaos' and 'mayhem'. This matched our observed assessment of the situation there. In private homes the situation varied, although staff groups tended to be more isolated from debates about the status of the profession and, consequently, tended to judge morale solely on the basis of their immediate situation.

It was also notable that different staff within the same team often had very different perceptions of the current state of morale within the home. Responses could therefore range from 'extremely low' to 'excellent' to 'not particularly high'. This contrasted with the assessments made by heads of home, who were distinctly more negative about the state of morale than other residential staff, though in a number of homes there was a sense that the situation was improving. Heads of homes in all areas linked low morale to the amount of change which the homes or the residential sector within the local authority had experienced. Unsurprisingly, they were also more conscious of the way in which low morale was reflected in high levels of sickness and staff absences.

Overall, and as might be expected, morale was frequently considered to be a shifting entity: 'up and down' was a common response. Staff were also aware of variations within the staff team. One residential social worker was more cynical still, commenting that, 'residential staff always have to have something to complain about'. But the factors related to low morale tended to be consistent generally across the different categories of home. A sense of insecurity, related to uncertainty about a specific unit, or even the future of residential care in an authority, was considered to be important both by heads of home and residential social workers. This was especially notable for staff in North, where three of the five homes had been subject to a series of delays in decisions about moving to new premises. Instability in the staff group was also perceived to be an important factor, especially in South where considerable restructuring had taken place and greater use was made of temporary staff. Staff in two of the private homes acknowledged that recent intakes of staff meant that the group had yet to be consolidated and this affected general morale. However, while such conditions may contribute to low morale in a home, as we have seen this does not mean that problems will necessarily result.

Conclusion

Important changes have clearly affected staff in children's homes over the past decade. Most noticeably there are more of them in each home and staff now outnumber residents. No staff in the current study actually lived in or adjacent to the residential home, whereas this applied to virtually all heads of homes in the 1985 research, a quarter of local authority residential social workers and most of those working in the private sector. The meaning of the work has therefore changed and the public and private selves are more distinct. This may have diminished the vocational element of the work, which has been historically very important, and has both advantages and disadvantages. Other changes seem to indicate more men involved in residential child care work than hitherto, an interesting development. Our sample of staff is also an older group than previously. It is conjecture, but this could have been caused by fewer younger recruits entering the work or the ambitious choosing to leave as homes closed. The withdrawal of single-person accommodation may also have deterred some from starting their careers in the residential sector. Nonetheless, the current staff group has considerable experience of child care work, although it has had to move around frequently to achieve this. Levels of professional qualifications, though an improvement on the 1980s, remain pitifully low. Some improvement in the status of the work has been perceived but it remains an undervalued area of activity.

Several of the findings in this chapter echo other material contained in the report. Heads of homes and others were critical of current organisational structures in social services departments. Staff complained of frequent restructuring. External management was felt to provide little support. As our observations in homes revealed, young people are a complex and difficult-to-manage group and most staff were unsure exactly how they should be going about this.

Against this general background, important differences have nevertheless emerged from the two local authorities running residential homes, North and South. We saw earlier that North had introduced a greater degree of specialisation for its units, which led to clearer objectives. It has now been indicated that North was more likely to allow its homes to keep to these objectives and not, for example, be pressurised into admitting inappropriate referrals. We have also discovered that North had better staffing ratios than South, a much more committed approach to qualifying training, more stable staffing groups and enjoyed better staff morale. It will be interesting to examine whether these factors are linked with more positive experiences for children living in its residential homes.

Summary points

- Staffing ratios have improved considerably since 1985: on this occasion there were more staff than residents in our 12 homes. There has also been an increase in the proportion of male residential workers.

- The number of staff with professional social work qualifications has increased since 1985 but still stands at only one in six. Four of the 11 heads of homes interviewed were professionally qualified. Thirteen per cent of staff were university graduates, the same proportion as previously.

- Overall, staff are now a much more experienced group compared with the earlier study, with an average of seven rather than three years' experience. However, many had changed jobs frequently: 6 of the 11 heads of homes had joined their current unit within the past 12 months. Greater staffing stability was evident in North compared with South, which also had higher staffing ratios and a more committed approach to qualifying training, together with other positive factors.

- Staff were critical of the constant restructuring of services in local authorities. Little external management support was provided to homes.

- Staff were convinced that in recent years young people admitted to homes had become more complex and difficult to manage. Homes in North were allowed to keep to their agreed referral criteria but in South this was not possible to the same degree.

- Some improvement in the status of residential child care within social work was felt to have occurred, but it remains very low. Its standing in local neighbourhoods and society at large was thought to be as weak as ever.

- Widespread differences in experiences and practices have emerged between the 12 homes. Staff morale was found to vary considerably across homes and was related to both external and internal factors. Assessment of the state of morale varied between staff in the same home.

7

Quality of Care in Children's Homes

It was explained in Chapter 2 that we designed this study to be more evaluative than its predecessor. This is part of a broader trend in child welfare research in which, now that there has been a reasonable amount of 'mapping' of the field and we have a better idea of children's and families' characteristics and experiences (Department of Health and Social Security 1985), we can try to identify common elements of good practice and good outcomes (Parker *et al.* 1991). There is also greater political and professional emphasis on accountability and value for money.

We described earlier how we came to abandon our original approach, which was to have used the Assessment and Action Records of the Department of Health's (1995b) *Looking After Children* package. Having now read some of our findings about the occupants of homes, the use of residential care and certain care practices, readers may have a better idea of why we encountered problems.

We thus decided to change our approach and, rather than focus on outcomes for individual children, sought to define instead what we felt were key areas of residential practice and to 'measure' the quality of care in each. This of course rather begs the question of whether good practices necessarily lead to good outcomes, and we were fortunate here in being able to draw on a detailed study of this topic at the University of York (Sinclair and Gibbs 1996). We turn to their results later. There are also questions about appropriate time-scales for ascertaining outcomes and, although we usually take a medium- or long-term view, it can be argued that children should be entitled to positive experiences *each day*. Hence, as far as the child is concerned, service inputs may themselves be regarded as 'outcomes' of a sort (Parker *et al.* 1991). From this perspective, there are large elements of consensus in authoritative texts on the practise of residential child care (Department of Health 1991b; Kahan 1994), and our approach incorporated a number of these ideas.

Our scrutiny of the quality of care in children's homes was based on the participant observation described earlier as well as some interview material. There is therefore much evaluative evidence in Chapter 5 on care practices, in the form of qualitative data. This is valuable in providing detailed insight into the processes involved in children's homes. However, we also wanted to provide 'harder' data and to try to measure the quality of care using statistical techniques. In certain key areas, therefore, we converted some of the qualitative data into a quantitative format. This was done immediately on return from the fieldwork visit to each children's home, so that events were fresh. We also used the extensive notes from our participant observations. The two researchers worked collaboratively on these ratings, thus providing a form of verification.

Statistical analysis was undertaken using Microsoft Excel and SPSS-X (Bryman and Cramer 1990; Kinnear and Gray 1994). A note of caution should be introduced here. Our sample of homes is obviously not large and we should be cautious about seeking to generalise from the results. This applies even more to sub-categories. Indeed for this sample size, correlations (Pearson coefficient), for example, will need to approach levels of almost $r = .6$ to achieve statistical significance and before we can become more confident, therefore, about the reliability of the measurement (Clarke and Cooke 1983). We hope that our results will suggest hypotheses for others and encourage more detailed inquiry.

The exact process for researcher ratings for each home was as follows. We identified 13 key areas of practice, set out in Table 7.1. In these, we jointly 'scored' the observed quality of care for each home on a scale of 0–10: the higher the score the more positive the evaluation. In fact this was done to one decimal point and so, effectively, the scale being used was 0–100. The exact procedure was, for each variable, to draw a line 10 centimetres long and to mark on it where we felt the home should score on that particular item. In each case, one of the two researchers had personally undertaken the participant observation in the home and, therefore, took the lead in suggesting the rating to be allocated. However, the second researcher had also visited, sometimes more than once. In addition we made use of the detailed structured notes we had written based on our visits. The ratings to be allocated were thus discussed and negotiated.

Quality-of-care variables

The 13 key variables selected, together with a brief description of each, are set out in Table 7.1. Inevitably there is some overlap.

Richard Titmuss alleged that one of the best indicators of the level of service provided by social security offices was the quality of toilet facilities for the public: their cleanliness, decoration and lighting (Abel-Smith and Titmuss 1987)! We did not include this in our study, although he may well have been right. Instead, the selection of the following criteria was influenced by our particular concerns within this research; therefore elements such as care planning or child protection were not prioritised. Common ground intentionally exists with the 1985 investigation. In addition, there is overlap with an evaluation scale to measure the quality of short-term care services for disabled children (Robinson, Weston and Minkes 1996).

Table 7.1 Quality-of-care variables used in the study

1. Quality of relationships between staff and young people
The quality of interactions between staff and residents. Do staff appear to be warm and caring? Do they spend time with children individually? Do children talk to them about their concerns and problems?

2. Degree of staff involvement with young people
The amount of time staff spend with residents rather than doing other duties.

3. Child-centred or institution-oriented
The balance of staff attention between children and their needs, and maintenance of the organisation. Does the smooth running of the home become an end in itself?

4. Adequacy of educational environment
Is the children's home a stimulating learning environment? Are there, and do staff encourage the use of, books, magazines, newspapers, comics, games and toys? Are television and video used educationally? Do staff take children out to places of interest?

5. Care for minority ethnic groups
Is attention paid to issues of culture, religion and language? Does the composition of the staff team reflect the ethnicity of residents? Is there variety in food and music? Are there links with minority communities?

6. Young people's involvement
Are children involved in the running of the home? Are they consulted about important issues? Are there young people's meetings?

7. Control problems
To what extent are there problems of behavioural management both inside and outside the home? How often are physical restraints used?

8. Staff morale
Do staff seem to enjoy their work and being with children? How often do they appear dissatisfied, especially in the presence of children?

9. Focus of staff concerns on narrow or wider issues
Do staff lose sight of the overall objectives of their work with individual children? Are they unduly preoccupied with events within the children's home? Do they develop longer-term perspectives?

10. Emphasis on family contact
Are staff positively disposed towards parents and other relatives? Do they take measures to enhance relationships between children and families?

11. Community links
Do external figures visit the children's homes? Do children have and maintain friends outside the children's home? Do children take part in community activities, such as sports clubs, visits to leisure and recreation facilities, youth clubs, discos and so on?

12. Relationships with social workers
Have staff developed positive relationships with children's social workers? How much involvement do the latter demonstrate?

13. Relationships with external professionals
To what extent have relationships developed, and how useful are they perceived to be, with the police, education and health professionals?

Each of the above 13 variables would no doubt justify a research study in itself. Readers may question the inclusion of some of these categories. For example, there is the 'control problems' variable. We decided to add this because homes that are frequently in conflict have less time to address children's wider needs; alternatively, of course, they may experience fewer behavioural problems if those needs are met in the first place. Confrontational children also monopolise staff attention and the subdued can be neglected. Though it may spark off excitement in some, other children described feelings of anxiety and insecurity when there were major disputes, possibly reminiscent of violence and other incidents at home. Similarly, we also felt that 'staff morale' should be included in our list. Though to some degree it might be considered an 'outcome' of other factors, staff attitudes and responsiveness have a major influence on children's residential experiences. In the home with probably the greatest problems in our sample (E), staff frequently retreated to an office and made themselves unavailable to young people. Morale here was desperately low.

Quality of care in homes

Using the listing of homes outlined in Chapter 4 and the numbering of variables from Table 7.1, our results on the quality of care demonstrated in homes are shown in Table 7.2.

Several interesting points emerge from the data presented in Table 7.2. First, it is immediately apparent that there is much variation in ratings. There are five individual scores of 9.6 from three different homes: in fact home F obtained three separate scores at this level. In contrast, homes E and C obtained only 0.3 and 0.4 respectively for the adequacy of their educational environments. The extent of variation is reflected in the high standard deviations for certain categories, particularly (4) educational environment (2.9); (12) relationships with social workers (2.0); and (9) focus of staff concerns on narrow or wider issues (2.3). There was more similarity in scores, and lower standard deviations, in relation to (1) the quality of relationships between staff and young people (1.0); and (3) whether homes were child-centred or institution-oriented (1.4). The quality of care for all 12 homes combined, reflected in the column averages (means), was quite high in relation to staff relationships with young people: variables 1–3 scored 8.1, 7.5 and 7.4. In contrast, the sample was much less impressive on educational environment (average 3.5) and control problems (4.5). Somewhat worryingly, homes scored higher for their relationships with external professionals (6.9) than with social workers (6.4)! These results are consistent with the qualitative data presented in Chapter 5.

The final column calculates an average score for each home across all 13 variables. The most impressive overall figure applied to short breaks home I in Borough, which obtained 8.5. Home F for younger children in North was next

Table 7.2 Quality of care in children's homes

Quality-of-care variables	1	2	3	4	5	6	7	8	9	10	11	12	13	Overall
Home														
Adolescents														
A	6.5	6.0	5.2	0.7	n.a	3.3	5.2	6.7	5.1	8.4	9.4	7.8	7.4	6.0
B	9.6	7.7	8.6	3.0	n.a	6.5	6.8	8.3	9.1	6.3	9.5	5.1	8.2	7.4
C	7.9	6.3	7.2	0.4	n.a	7.2	6.1	6.1	5.2	7.6	5.0	7.0	5.1	5.9
D	9.3	4.9	7.4	0.9	n.a	5.3	3.1	6.8	9.1	9.1	9.2	6.2	6.2	6.5
E	6.9	3.9	4.4	0.3	n.a	5.2	1.2	3.2	3.2	6.0	2.7	2.3	6.0	3.8
Young children														
F	9.5	9.6	9.3	7.7	n.a	8.5	5.1	9.6	9.5	4.1	9.3	9.3	9.6	8.4
G	7.5	8.0	8.1	3.2	n.a	5.1	2.3	5.9	4.5	6.9	5.2	5.9	6.6	5.8
Short breaks														
H	8.1	8.4	7.8	1.8	n.a	5.6	8.6	5.6	3.4	4.0	2.2	6.4	8.2	5.8
I	9.0	9.4	7.7	8.2	9.6	8.0	4.2	8.8	9.4	8.7	9.3	9.3	9.4	8.5
Private homes														
J	7.7	8.3	8.0	6.1	5.0	7.7	3.6	6.0	7.5	4.3	7.7	3.9	5.9	6.3
K	7.7	9.5	8.1	3.0	3.4	5.0	4.1	4.8	7.0	6.6	5.0	5.1	4.2	5.7
L	7.4	8.4	7.1	6.1	6.6	6.4	3.2	6.5	6.1	8.9	5.8	6.1	6.3	6.5
Column average	8.1	7.5	7.4	3.5	6.2	6.2	4.5	6.5	6.6	6.7	6.7	6.2	6.9	6.4
Standard deviation	1.0	1.9	1.4	2.9	2.6	1.5	2.0	1.7	2.3	1.9	2.7	2.0	1.7	1.3
Correlation total score	.75	.64	.69	.75	–	.65	.34	.97	.82	.06	.74	.77	.70	–

Note: There were no children from minority ethnic groups in homes A–H; 'n.a.' means not applicable.

Table 7.3 Distribution of 'good', 'average' and 'poor' homes

	North	South	Borough	Adoles-cent	Young children	Short breaks	Private	All homes
Good (7+)	2	0	1	1	1	1	0	3
Average (4–6)	3	2	0	3	1	1	3	8
Poor (<4)	0	1	0	1	0	0	0	1
TOTAL	5	3	1	5	2	2	3	12

with 8.4. The highest score for an adolescent home was 7.4 for B, while for the private sector it was L with 6.5. The lowest figure by a noticeable margin was only 3.8 for E, followed interestingly by G for younger children and the other short-term care home H, both with 5.8. As groups, those offering short breaks and younger children's homes scored highest (7.2 and 7.1, though there was variation within them), while adolescent and private homes were quite similar (5.9, 6.2). The average figure for homes in North was noticeably higher (7.3) than those in South (5.3).

We could translate these results into more readily understood language by creating categories of 'good', 'average' and 'poor' homes, with mean scores respectively of 7 or above, 4–6 and below 4 (Table 7.3). On this basis, a quarter of our homes – 3 of the 12 – would be 'good'. One of the 12 would be 'poor', but the largest group – two-thirds of homes – would be 'average'. Results on the quality of care for the private homes as a group fell in between those for the two local authorities.

The major conclusion from these results seems to us to be not so much concern about the overall standard of residential practice but about its *unevenness*. This point arose also in Chapter 5. Some homes do quite well, yet most are just middling. At least there are more 'good' than 'poor' homes. It is also important to note that the four homes that score highest (I, F, B and L) come from different categories. This suggests that it is not merely that there are some groups of residents to whom it is easier to deliver effective services than others. Indeed, there is more variation *within* the categories than *between* them. It is also interesting to observe that there is not a particularly strong link between the severity of young people's problems and the quality of care offered within homes. As discussed in Chapter 4, calculating the average number of 'major stress factors' for young people resident, there is only a low negative relationship ($r = -.41$) between this and the quality of care.

While regretting the fact that the overall quality of care is not higher, these findings nevertheless give grounds for optimism. They suggest that presumably there is no intrinsic reason why good quality care cannot be delivered to problematic children. Some homes in our sample offered an effective service to very difficult young people in complex circumstances, yet others did not. We turn later to some of the main factors in homes that seemed to be preconditions for delivering high quality care.

First, however, we make three further observations. One is that in Table 7.2 we can see that there is quite a high degree of consistency across variables, and homes that are strong in some areas tend also to achieve high scores in others: in the bottom row it is shown that correlations of individual columns with the total average score are generally high. There are two exceptions to this. One relates to the severity of control problems, where some homes that came out well overall nevertheless had serious problems in managing behaviour. A good example of this was with the short breaks home for disabled children – I – which scored highest overall but was below average regarding control. The other exception concerns emphasis on family contact. This could be attributable to the fact that there were court orders prohibiting contact for some children. In addition, the short breaks homes were sometimes ambivalent about family contact, feeling that for family members a complete break was often advisable and necessary. The effects on residents were considered unfortunate but unavoidable. It should be remembered, of course, that these placements were for a week's duration.

A second observation on the results depicted in Table 7.2 is that we had previously asked managers when interviewed to rank homes used by their children according to the quality of care delivered (see Chapter 3). We explained broadly the sorts of criteria by which we would be making our judgements. It appeared to us an interesting exercise to examine the degree of agreement. Once the homes are divided between local authorities we are obviously dealing with very small numbers. The situation may also change over time within homes (Whitaker *et al*. 1996). Nonetheless, it emerged that there was only a slight overlap between managers' rankings and our own. In North the manager agreed with us on the home that scored highest but placed as last of his five the one that we put second. If anything the situation was worse in South, where the manager ranked bottom of their three the one we had placed highest: our results were almost the reverse of one another. Ironically, the manager who according to our criteria was best informed was in Borough, who seemed better acquainted with private sector homes than were our other two managers with their own provision! We were surprised that our perceptions were so very different. It did not seem to us, therefore, that managers had a very good understanding of the patterns of care and dynamics within homes.

An additional point in relation to Table 7.2 concerns staff morale, which reveals a remarkably high relationship with overall quality of care in homes ($r = .97$). Admittedly this was quite a complex variable to gauge, but staff morale and staff perceptions appear from this to be a barometer, almost, of care practice. Though we did not explore in any depth the issue of staff sub-cultures, and there are of course matters of cause and effect, this finding could also be seen as consistent with other research that has demonstrated the importance of congruence between the formal goals of children's homes and staff (and children's) cultures (Brown *et al.* forthcoming). An interesting corollary was that our data show no simple direct relationship between staff morale and the control problems a home is experiencing ($r = .36$). In the right circumstances, staff can remain positively motivated even when confronted by very difficult children. Indeed, we suggested in Chapter 6 that the level of morale stems from a complex interplay of external and internal factors.

Factors associated with the quality of care

Having discussed various indicators of the quality of care, the next step is to explore what appear to be the associated factors. If we can determine what elements are present in homes that deliver an effective service, one would hope to be able to raise standards elsewhere by replicating some of them. However, we should first issue another cautionary note about the use and interpretation of statistical measurements of correlation. Simply because two factors are associated does not, of course, mean that one necessarily causes the other: social science students are often reminded that there is a very strong correlation between the number of fire officers present at a blaze and the damage it inflicts, but they are, hopefully, trying to put it out rather than responsible for the ruin.

We began this analysis by examining a number of structural variables and seeing whether they were linked to the overall measure of quality of care provided in homes. This produced some surprising results and none in fact demonstrated strong associations. We should be careful how these findings are interpreted, a point to which we return below. Hence we discovered virtually no relationship between staffing ratios and quality of care ($r = -.07$). The two homes with the most favourable staffing ratios (H and C) came out overall only ninth equal and eighth. It seems from our data, then, that there is no simple relationship between the quality of care provided in a home and the number of staff, which is the first explanation that is often provided.

Similar results occurred when we considered the professional qualifications of staff, though here we examined only qualifying training rather than the quite extensive range of in-house courses that is now more often provided. Here we found that the home that came first (I) and the two that were fourth equal (D and L) had *no* staff who were professionally qualified in social work. The overall correlation between staff qualifications and quality of care provided was low ($r = .34$). An interesting pattern was discovered when we analysed the extent of social work qualifications among heads of homes. With only one exception, home D – which actually came out second best in its group – all heads of adolescent and young children's homes were professionally qualified. This compares with no heads of the short breaks or private homes holding qualifications. Quality of care was unrelated to the professional qualifications of heads of home *per se* ($r = .04$).

Unexpectedly, we found a low *negative* correlation between quality of care in homes and the proportion of university or college graduates on staff groups ($r = -.41$), suggesting at face value that better educated staff can be detrimental to good care! Though, as we saw in the previous chapter, the number of graduates in total was quite sparse, none were employed in homes that came in the top four (I, F, B and D). There was also only a weak relationship between the care provided and experience of staff ($r = .35$).

We need to be clear about what all this means, particularly as very similar findings have arisen in a recent quantitative study with a larger sample than ours (Sinclair and Gibbs 1996). It would be a serious misinterpretation, in our opinion, if it were to be felt that it is unnecessary, for example, to have adequate numbers of staff, provide them with relevant training and to value experience. However, the point is that *in themselves* these useful measures are no guarantee that good quality care will automatically result. It would be rather simplistic to have assumed otherwise. The point is that these measures may have other benefits. They may contribute indirectly to better care for children. They may have complex relationships with other variables that we have not so far considered or which we do not understand. There is also a difference between gathering data *cross-sectionally* and *longitudinally*. For example, in another study we discovered that children's homes that increased staffing over time, as part of a wider strategy, were thought to have improved their service (Berridge *et al.* 1995). However, the clear message from the current research is that there are more effective ways of improving residential care than merely increasing staffing and relying on qualifying training.

So let us search more widely. For the next stage of the analysis we included additional quantitative data derived from our interviews with heads of homes, other staff and children, and participant observation. This totalled over 50 independent variables, which we checked against the overall quality of care score for each home. Initially, we computed correlation coefficients to examine the strength of individual variables. Once again this highlighted areas that were not directly linked to our quality-of-care measurements, including heads of homes' attitudes to the current management structure ($r = -.12$) and whether they felt they received adequate management support ($r = -.14$).

Children's perceptions

We would expect some factors to be highly correlated with quality of care and, reassuringly, this emerged from our data. These serve, therefore, to validate our conceptual and methodological approach. For example, there was a strong association between quality of care and *staff* assessment of morale in homes

$(r = .73)$ (this is different from the combined variable included in Table 7.2). But it was also interesting to observe that *children's perceptions* of the contribution of homes were broadly consistent with our own evaluations $(r = .59)$. These were obtained essentially through asking residents an open-ended question. As we saw in Chapter 5, relationships between staff and residents were generally positive. If anything, staff were withdrawing from interaction with children rather than the reverse. In addition to general conversations and opportunistic exchanges during our visits to homes, we managed to hold longer individual discussions with about half the residents in adolescent and private homes. We kept these flexible as boredom thresholds varied. Conversations with younger children were more general and usually took place in group settings, perhaps while playing a game. Keyworkers and other staff often encouraged children to tell us their thoughts, write something down or draw a picture.

Obtaining the views of children with severe learning disabilities would have required an even more specialist approach, as reflected in the useful work of Robinson *et al.* (1996). Most had limited communication. It may be possible to infer perceptions about the residential experience from certain of children's gestures and reactions. Certainly in home I, for example, there were some outward signs of distress on departure from the home and not just on arrival. Outings by foot or minibus eagerly set off. Appetites were mostly extensive, there was much laughter and children frequently held, cuddled and sat on members of staff. There were also of course negative experiences, for example one young woman with limited mobility was repeatedly intimidated by another hurtful female resident.

For researchers as with other professionals, trying to ascertain children's genuine beliefs can be problematic (Hill *et al.* 1996; Spencer and Flyn 1990). They may give the answers they feel unfamiliar adults want to hear and be unsure of the consequences of critical statements. We tried to prevent this as much as possible by the way that we prepared for the study (see Chapter 2). By spending several days in homes, and becoming acquainted with one another, some children talked to us towards the end of our visits who otherwise might not have done. We could also observe young people's interactions with staff and overhear some of their conversations.

With this in mind, the overwhelming majority of comments from residents in adolescent and younger children's homes were positive about their staff. They said they were caring, understanding and prepared to listen to young people and try to help them with their problems. For adolescents, unfortunately, one fears that this may often be an all too brief interlude between less rewarding experiences (Sinclair and Gibbs 1996). An eight-year-old girl expressed it simply: 'Staff are kind'. Adolescents used terms such as, 'everyone's really friendly. You get a lot of support when you need it. You are close to them. They can sort things out for you. If I was one of the staff I'd crack up'.

Comments relating to private homes were, however, more mixed. There were still the positive endorsements such as, 'they're here to help. They help a lot', but this was balanced with more critical observations: 'All the new staff don't listen. They'd rather listen to their own voices'. We encountered probably only one young person in our study who was extremely hostile to her residential placement and staff group: 'Some of them listen but I really hate it here'.

Average scores that we attributed to children's expressed attitudes towards staff were 8.4 for adolescent homes, 8.7 with younger children and 6.2 in the three private homes. A low score was achieved in adolescent home E (5.7), which we have seen already was experiencing major problems. Here staff made themselves unavailable for long periods, retreating to the office and shutting the door. Residents hovered outside, moving to and fro, as if constantly attracted by some force. Reflecting on the nature of the private homes' population (Chapter 4), it is possible that the more complex and perhaps emotionally disturbed group that they sheltered were more likely to vent their anger on staff and the adult world in general. Indeed, some in the psychodynamic tradition might judge it a positive feature that children were able to be critical rather than repress their feelings (for example, Balbernie 1966). Staff in home E did not see it quite this way.

Other explanations for variations in children's views about staff could relate to regimes and staffing patterns. One private home that scored relatively poorly in this area (K – 5.8) adopted a highly supervisory role of young people's behaviour and activities. Children who went out into the local town always had to be accompanied by an adult. While this by and large maintained order in a very difficult group, some of whom were otherwise clear candidates for secure provision, the close scrutiny was not always appreciated by the young people concerned.

In addition, as shown in Chapter 6, the greater dissatisfaction with staffing in the private homes may have been because there were fewer of them. Staff in private homes were also expected to do more of the cooking and other domestic duties, whereas local authorities usually employed separate ancillary staff. While these tasks could be undertaken jointly with children or at least in their company, it nevertheless reduced the amount of direct child care work that staff in private homes were able to undertake.

Other factors

A series of further statistical exercises was undertaken to explore the association between variables and the quality of care offered in homes. Several factors emerged which proved to be important. These included the extent to which the head of home was able to state specific objectives for the home ($r = .64$), could keep to the main objectives ($r = .71$), had some say in admissions ($r = .67$) and, strongest of all, could articulate a clear theoretical/therapeutic orientation or specific methods of work for caring for children ($r = .82$). This last variable has a strong link with the second and third of these points ($r = .66, .71$), but the correlation with the first, the head of home's ability to specify objectives, is interestingly lower ($r = .39$). On its own, the capacity to define a specific orientation or methods of work accounted for some two-thirds of variation in the quality of care demonstrated in our 12 homes.

Orientation and methods of work

We saw in Chapter 5 that most of our homes did not have completed Statements of Purpose and that, even where they did exist, the depiction of the exact clientele and objectives for homes was rather vague. The same applied to methods of work. We were not necessarily expecting elaborate accounts of the work of Jung, Freud or other eminent figures, but we did hope to find some sort of thought-out therapeutic approach. At the very least, we hoped for clear methods of work and some internal systems around them.

Regrettably this was to be the exception rather than the rule. Orientation and working methods were most vague in the five adolescent homes, to most of which it was difficult to allocate many points at all in our evaluation system. One home had been intended to offer a therapeutic service but the current resident group was felt to have made this impossible. An adolescent home in North was due to close and there were clearer plans to offer a more specific community-based programme of accommodation and support. However, two of the adolescent homes saw it as a positive advantage that they had no specific working methods but instead, almost, made it up as they went along. One head of home justified this with the statement: 'We prefer to work with young people as individuals'. Another felt it would be dangerous to have a theoretical approach to child care with an untrained staff group: we would argue the opposite. Heads of three of the adolescent homes commented that young people themselves should set the agenda for work with them: 'We basically work to the individual – we let them set the agenda'. Another remarked: 'If you formalise things they feed you what you want to hear'. Working in partnership with adolescents is not the same as outright self-determination (Department of Health 1996c; Sinclair et al. 1995). This has dangerous implications for young people's safety, as we saw in Chapter 5. The York research signalled also the extent to which residential work was determined by young people's motivation (Sinclair and Gibbs 1996).

There was generally a clearer view of working methods in other categories of home, but about half were still extremely vague. There were, however, some exceptions. The head of home for younger children that scored highly overall (F) described how they worked through the breakdown process with the child. Using previously developed practice tools, they undertook life story work and examined psychological attachments. Care plans figured prominently and the home had developed its own documentation system for planning and monitoring progress. One of the private homes (J) used a child psychiatrist and trained counsellor as consultants to help staff devise appropriate 'treatment plans': this was one of the rare occasions on which the phrase arose. Staff here had also undertaken counselling courses. Another private home (L) set out to provide therapeutic care in small family-like settings. In association with a specialist outside agency, it used play therapy techniques following an assessment of children's behavioural characteristics.

The other home with clearly thought through methods of work was the home in Borough for children with severe learning disabilities (I). This had clear written objectives. As with its counterpart in North, short-term care was used as a planned strategy of family support. There was a detailed assessment of all children in home I, both by fieldworkers and senior residential staff, prior to places being offered. Detailed care plans were drawn up for each child outlining health care, education and behaviour, to which parents, other professionals and residential staff adhered. Whereas in this home, therefore, they were generally singing to the same tune, elsewhere the song had often not been written and sometimes music was even discouraged.

This absence of a clear philosophy, particularly in adolescent homes, is a complex issue to which we return in our conclusion. It is difficult to develop a coherent approach in settings where objectives are not identified and sustained. It was disappointing in the absence of other explanations that heads of homes seldom referred to the principles of the Children Act 1989 and associated practice guidance as a starting point to establishing a coherent approach (though they often adhered to it in practice) (Department of Health 1991b). These problems are linked to the general dearth of theory in current residential child care which has been remarked on elsewhere (Bullock *et al.* 1993). It relates to debates about the role of theory in social work more generally. This has been analysed from the perspective of newly qualified staff (Marsh and Triseliotis 1996), in relation to 'reflective practice' (Gould 1989; Schön 1983) and in conditions of '(post) modernity' (Parton 1994). Once there was a strong religious orientation to residential services and an explicit 'rescue' philosophy. Theories have since come and gone but in many of our homes staff were not provided with a coherent explanation of children's problems and behaviour, and a method or methods by which this could be addressed. There are fundamental dilemmas about the meaning and purpose of residential care for adolescents. None of this is helped by the wider and future problems of residents: the marginalisation of youth, more punitive attitudes towards the young, the collapse of the job market for unskilled working-class adolescents and the 'ghettoisation' of some urban areas (Pitts forthcoming). Faced elsewhere with serious disorder and attrition, one can perhaps begin to understand why regimes such as 'Pindown' had their attractions to otherwise benign staff (Levy and Kahan 1991). Any theory is more attractive than no theory at all in helping to bring about a coherent culture.

As a final observation in this section, we should remind ourselves that information on orientation and working methods was derived from our interviews with heads of homes. Rather than focusing specifically on detailed content, therefore, what we may actually be evaluating are the ability and skills of heads of homes (together with managers or senior staff) to articulate, develop and introduce an overall framework for residential child care in their establishment. As shown earlier, we did not find strong relationships between the quality of care offered and professional and educational qualifications of heads of homes and staff. But thinking of the three homes that scored highly in relation to their orientation and methods of work (I, F and L), each had a head of home or proprietor who demonstrated leadership and impressed us as a manager and practitioner. Yet the same could be said of one other head of home which did not score well in relation to orientation and methods of work, although the home was about to close and there was a clearer vision for the future service. She also had not been in post very long. We are unable to take this argument much further, but it would be useful for future research on residential care to focus specifically on the skills and practices of heads of homes and relate these to the overall quality of care and outcomes for children. An earlier study of probation hostels discovered that wardens' characteristics influenced success rates (Sinclair 1971).

Staffing stability

Clarity in orientation and methods of work, therefore, was the main factor accounting for variation in the quality of care in the sample of 12 homes. However, another variable that emerged as important was, interestingly, stability in staffing. We saw in Chapter 6 that the average (median) time that staff had been working at homes was some 2.5 years. This ranged from over 4.5 years in the two short breaks homes down to nearer 1 year in the private facilities. Homes for adolescents and younger children came in between (2 years 1 month, 1 year 8 months). Heads of homes had often joined more recently.

There was greater staffing stability in homes in North compared with South, which as we have seen generally achieved better quality of care scores. This may have been due to the more positive training and secondment policy and a greater commitment to residential care, as well as a lack of alternative employment opportunities. One might also expect there to be higher staff turnover at homes in crisis. This certainly applied to home E, where half the staff were recent arrivals, and at D which had also experienced considerable difficulties including a recent bereavement.

It could be argued that too much staffing stability in a children's home, like a university department, is a weakness rather than a strength, as able and ambitious colleagues transfer to more senior and interesting posts elsewhere. Obviously homes occasionally need fresh faces, ideas and abilities. On the other hand, it is important to nurture employees, develop skills and to establish team relationships and working practices over time. Linking this to the previous point, it is impossible to convey a framework for practice and associated working methods if staff are constantly changing (let alone heads of homes and organisational structures). Most importantly, perhaps, though many residents do not stay for long, a sense of stability and continuity are important. An established staff group is also better positioned to develop an ethos whereby behavioural norms can be sustained.

Conclusion: comparisons with other research

Our statistical analysis, therefore, revealed strong links between quality of care and the extent to which the head of home could state specific objectives for the establishment, could keep to them and, as a corollary, had some say in admissions. However, two factors emerged as particularly important: first, the ability of the head of home to articulate a clear theoretical/therapeutic orientation or specific methods of work; and, second, stability in the staff group. On this basis, homes are effective when they develop clear methods of work, provide continuity and nurture members of staff and staff teams. How does this compare with the results from other studies?

Colton (1988) undertook one of the most detailed studies of residential child care, when he compared groups of children's homes and specialist foster homes. The focus was more on actual care practices than their determinants. Nonetheless, the study suggested that an important influence on practice in children's homes, in contrast to foster care, was 'bureaucratisation', including the hierarchical structure, system of rules and regulations, specialised division of labour and impersonal social relations. We did not specifically investigate these features, but it would not appear from our results that the homes that did better were necessarily less bureaucratic than others. For example, private homes were not part of local authority bureaucratic structures yet their quality of care was not noticeably superior: one home (L) came out well but two others (J and K) did not. Furthermore home I, which scored highest, was probably among the most bureaucratic: it had a clear hierarchical structure, different categories of staff – night staff, cooks, cleaners, administrative assistant, caretaker and so on; and there was extensive use of written information. In contrast, a greater degree of structure would have been welcomed in home E, which was more anomic than bureaucratic. Interestingly, however, 'the office' became the major staff focal point, which is a strong bureaucratic feature.

The other major research study relevant to ours, by Sinclair and Gibbs (1996), has already been referred to several times. Their work concluded that three main factors were associated with their definition of 'goodhome':

Homes are more easily kept in reasonable shape if:

- they are small;

- the head of home feels that its roles are clear, mutually compatible, and not disturbed by frequent reorganisation and that he or she is then given adequate autonomy to get on with the job;

- the staff are agreed about how the home should run and are not at odds with each other (p.320).

We adopted a different approach to our work and may not be using concepts in the same way; however, let us compare results. We agree with the York research that variables such as staffing ratios and the level of professional qualifications are not in themselves related to measurements of the quality of care in individual homes. We also found that intake is not the main determinant of quality of care. However, in our study size of home was not a key factor ($r = .19$). In fact our largest home (I – 11 residents) was also the most impressive, while the three smallest (A, C and L – each with 4 young people) came seventh, eighth and fourth, respectively. The York calculations of size were based on the number of beds in homes, while for our analysis we used the number of residents: however, as occupancy rates were high this should not really make a difference. But an important point in our study is that *all* of our homes tended to be relatively small. In the York study 7 of the 39 homes had more than 10 places whereas we had just the one. It was these larger homes that came out worst on the York 'goodhome' measures, while there was less difference between those that were small and medium-sized.

Our results are consistent with the second and third York points. Clarity of role and working methods as well as 'empowerment' of the head of home also emerged as important in our study. We did not explore the effects of reorganisations. However, we saw the interesting difference between the previous experience of staff and duration in current post. Closure of homes and restructuring had influenced stability in staffing. We also saw earlier that staff morale, which was strongly linked to the quality of care, was affected by job insecurity and other external developments. Regarding autonomy, it was interesting in our findings that we did not discover a link between management support received by the head of home and quality of care, which is contrary to what one might have expected. Turning to the third York point – staff consensus – we did not approach this in the same way. However, our results do show quite a high relationship between quality of care and the extent to which the head of home and staff were in agreement on policy and practice issues. Continuity and, specifically, stability in the staffing group, may enhance this.

In sum, then, it strikes us that there is much overlap between our results and those of our colleagues from York. This is despite the fact that the projects were undertaken independently, had a different focus and involved quite distinct research methods.

Postscript: child protection

We conclude this chapter with a brief reference to the issue of child safety. The physical and sexual abuse of children living in residential institutions continues to be a matter of major public concern. Indeed, as this study has progressed, new revelations of malpractice have occurred in north Wales, Cardiff and north-west England to name but a few. Consequently, the government announced a review by Sir William Utting of the safeguards for children living away from home. Although a range of studies on residential care is currently in progress, it is interesting that few of them concentrate on issues of child safety. Exceptions are the work of Elaine Farmer (University of Bristol) and Christine Barter (National Society for the Prevention of Cruelty to Children/University of Luton; forthcoming 1997). In contrast the problem of institutional abuse has received more attention in the USA (see Blatt 1992). Child protection was not a focus of our work, although if one were commencing now it would need a higher profile – for example, by being a constituent variable in ascertaining the overall quality of care provided in homes.

However, having undertaken our detailed fieldwork and analysis, we would offer the following observations. Some of this may be interpreted in different ways. Several of our findings seem to us positive and to suggest increased protection from physical and sexual abuse for children living in residential homes. Thus children speak very positively of staff. Homes are now much smaller than they were a decade ago. Staffing ratios have improved. Children have more contact with families and length of stay in residential homes is shorter. Generally speaking, there is also greater age differentiation between homes and, therefore, less scope for younger children to be victimised by older adolescents. No staff now live in.

Other findings, however, could have the opposite implications. The resident group is more complex and more difficult to control. There is greater known prior experience of physical and sexual abuse. Disconcertingly, we saw that staff are unaware of the child protection status of several residents. Children receive very little specialist therapeutic help. Some homes are located in unsafe high-crime areas and staff are insufficiently vigilant about residents going out, especially late at night. Over the past decade the degree of external management of homes has diminished. Adolescents are frequently absent from school: this gives rise to opportunities for exploitation during unstructured times of the day, as well as removing the vital screening role of teachers and other education professionals. Levels of professional qualifications among staff in our sample had not altered greatly since 1985. Finally, without wishing to condemn all men, we know that males are responsible for the majority of cases of institutional abuse (Berridge and Brodie 1996; Blatt 1992). Compared with our earlier study there has been a slight increase in the proportion of male staff: there were almost equal numbers of female and male staff working in private establishments, and more men than women working in the five adolescent homes although female residents were in a majority.

Overall, therefore, though important advances have been made, one could not conclude categorically that children's homes are safer environments in which to live than a decade ago. Hopefully other researchers and practitioners can be alert to the implications of these findings.

Summary points

- There was much variation in the quality of care between homes. Overall, homes scored highly concerning staff relationships with young people but much lower on the educational environment within homes.

- Three of our 12 homes were judged to be 'good', eight 'average' and one 'poor'. As groups, those offering short-term breaks and younger children's homes were considered to be most effective, while adolescent and private children's homes were quite similar.

- A major concern about the quality of care was its unevenness. The four homes that scored highest came from different categories. There was more variation within categories of home than between them.

- There was not a strong link between the severity of young people's problems and the quality of care offered within homes.

- Local authority managers seemed ill-informed about the quality of care in their establishments. The manager in Borough was better acquainted with private sector provision than were the other two social services managers with their own homes.

- Staff morale was very highly correlated with quality of care.

- A range of structural factors were unrelated to the quality of service offered by individual homes, including staffing ratios and professional qualifications of staff. Care should be taken in the interpretation of these findings.

- Children were overwhelmingly positive about staff in their homes, although there was a tendency for comments to be more mixed from residents in the three private homes.

- Several variables associated with the internal running of establishments were strongly related to the quality of care offered within homes, including the extent to which the head of home could state specific objectives for the home; could keep to the main objectives; and had some say over admissions. Two factors that emerged as particularly relevant were the ability of the head of home to express a clear theoretical/therapeutic orientation or specific methods of work for the home; and staffing stability. In relation to the former, most homes were vague, especially adolescent homes.

- Our research findings are generally consistent with the results from another major study of children's homes undertaken at the University of York (Sinclair and Gibbs 1996).

- Though some of the recent developments in residential care offer greater protection to children from physical, sexual and emotional abuse, other changes do not.

8

Conclusion

This final chapter rounds off the study and highlights what are felt to be the most important points, and their implications, arising from what we discovered. We shall not attempt a full overview of the report, especially as summary points have been provided at the end of each chapter. Instead, we shall add some general observations on the situation of children's homes at the end the twentieth century.

The study has been a follow-up of research undertaken in the 1980s, focusing on residential child care provided to children and young people in three local authorities. Original homes that were still open were revisited and those that had closed were substituted with others that reflected current patterns of use. We have investigated changes in the children's homes sector over a decade, including who lives in homes and why; who works there; how establishments are organised and run; links with families and other professionals; and the quality of care that homes provide.

It was revealed that considerable changes have affected children's homes over the past decade. Most noticeably, there are now far fewer of them than there were and the sector has more than halved in size. Therefore, the original sample of 20 homes was reduced to 12 on this occasion. Only 4 of the 20 were open 10 years later. Even more dramatically, just 4 of the 136 staff encountered in 1985 were still now residential child care workers with the same employer. The voluntary residential sector has reduced substantially, a major change in child welfare this century. Larger community homes with education and homes with observation and assessment facilities, often resembling 'total institutions' (Goffman 1968), are also now rare. Their former clientele, today, would be more likely to use small, local, open facilities and mainstream schools. As their residents were often among the older and more difficult youths looked after by social services, this has raised behavioural management issues for local children's homes and schools.

Homes are now half the size they were a decade ago, with an average of only about six or seven residents. Staffing ratios have improved considerably, with the consequence that homes usually have more staff than children. In some respects homes tend to be more specialist than they were, for example there is now a greater tendency towards age segregation. A noticeable feature of children's homes today is the frequent absence of sibling groups: in 1985 some 40 per cent of all residents were living with a brother or sister, whereas in the current study, for example, this applied to none of the occupants of the five adolescent homes.

Due to the contraction of the sector and the closure of the larger institutions, children's homes now accommodate a much more complex and difficult group of residents than hitherto. With the exception of the group of disabled children receiving short-term breaks, most young people had been seriously abused or neglected prior to separation from home. The majority had experienced multiple 'stress factors'. The proportion posing behavioural problems prior to entry had more than doubled compared with 1985. Most residents had been assessed as having special educational needs. Special schools and special units were more in evidence on this occasion, as were non-attendance at school and formal exclusion.

Interestingly, no staff themselves lived in the 12 homes, which was a common option in our first study. This marks a profound shift in the structure of residential care and has occurred without explicit discussion, including its impact on child care. It has happened for other reasons. Levels of qualifications among staff had increased over the decade, but this still left eight in every ten professionally unqualified. Our staff interviews and periods of participant observation in homes highlighted two major problems which had not been present in 1985 and which are inter-linked. First, there was a difficulty in securing access to schooling specifically for adolescents. Sometimes this was because of formal exclusion but, frequently, pupils were absent for other reasons. Residential staff often did not appreciate this distinction. Reforms to educational legislation and policy have contributed to this problem.

A second major issue in homes that had not emerged to the same degree in the first study was problems of behavioural control. Staff were unsure and lacked confidence in how to deal with young people's indiscipline. We demonstrated that this is a complex phenomenon: it varies between homes, staff members and indeed local authorities, and is not always a rational assessment of the difficulties that children cause. Nonetheless, it is a major impediment to practice in many homes. Its resolution lies in addressing certain other problems with residential care, which we discuss below.

Some developments over the decade were disconcerting. It was generally reported to us, and confirmed from our own independent evidence, that homes received less external management attention and support compared with the 1985 research. Local authorities have traditionally neglected their children's residential units (Department of Health 1992). However, the fact that the majority of these 12 homes did not have completed Statements of Purpose – three years after the legislation required them – is a serious failure. Admittedly a Statement in itself is simply a paper document and what is more important than its mere existence is what it contains and how this is implemented. Nonetheless, the absence of this documentation symbolised broader neglect. The diminution of external management is also quite remarkable given the number of widely publicised scandals that have emerged in the late 1980s and 90s concerning the physical and sexual abuse of residents by some staff. Lack of management oversight was a consistent feature of the crises (Berridge and Brodie 1996).

Another worrying development was residential homes' relationships with other professionals. These varied but, overall, we were surprised to be informed that residential staff had better relationships with external professionals than with a local authority's own social workers. Changes in organisational structures were felt to have exacerbated problems in liaison with fieldwork colleagues, especially 'purchaser–provider' divisions.

This may all sound rather pessimistic and we should not overlook the positive developments that have occurred in homes over the past decade. One of these concerns children's relationships with birth parents. The nature of residents has changed in important respects over the decade but, even if we exclude the short breaks group who were away from home only for a few days at a time, relationships with parents were noticeably stronger than in the 1985 study. Residential staff were certainly more positive about promoting contacts with birth parents, and to a lesser degree with other relatives, while appreciating the problems this could lead to, including parents' unreliability. Maintaining contact was still fraught with difficulty. Nevertheless, staff understood the likely benefits of such contact and, unlike in 1985, did not make adverse comments about parents. It thus seems that the 1980s programme of research and its dissemination (Department of Health and Social Security 1985); the Children Act 1989, prior consultation and volumes of guidance; and the training that local authorities have mounted on this complex topic have paid dividends. Major change can be achieved if a concerted effort is made – the same probably needs to occur in relation to residential child care more generally.

An important focus of the study has been to examine the quality of care provided in the 12 homes. Obviously this is not a large sample and we should be cautious before generalising more widely. However, as we have shown, our results are certainly consistent with other recent research on children's homes, which used quite different methods. The main conclusion to emerge from our scrutiny of the quality of care was its variation: it was not so much that standards of residential practice were inadequate but that they were very *uneven*. We have confirmed that good quality care can be provided given the right circumstances, which is something that has been known all along. We should also not overlook the fact that homes and staff within them were mostly popular with residents, although this of course depends on their expectations and prior experiences. Our overall assessment of the sample of homes was that 3 of the 12 were judged to be 'good', 8 'average' and 1 'poor'. The 1985 study did not approach matters in quite the same way and the resident group is now more damaged and difficult; nonetheless, for the record, the group of homes then would probably have fallen within the three categories in more equal numbers. Over the decade, therefore, it appears that there are fewer 'good' and 'poor' homes but more of an 'average' quality. If more children are being protected from poor practice this must be seen as a step forward.

Our detailed examination of the quality of care yielded further interesting information. No single category of home had a monopoly over good (or poor) practice. The four 'best' homes came from the four different groups: therefore, for example, some homes were effective at working with adolescents. There was more variation in the care offered *within* categories of home than between them. Furthermore, the quality of care delivered was not directly related to the nature and extent of residents' problems. All of this seems to us very important and indicates that it is possible to deliver effective residential care to children. Young people do not in any way predetermine what professionals can provide. There are more important explanations which account for variations in practice.

Several factors were found to lead to high quality care, independently of other variables. For example, it was important for homes to have a clear sense of their objectives and to be able to keep to them. Having some say over admissions was part of this. Ineffective homes that we visited often sheltered all and sundry and some residents' needs and tasks that were required to be undertaken seemed mutually exclusive. Managers discouraged or prohibited these homes from becoming more selective, which solved their short-term accommodation needs but little else. We found no direct link between quality of care and staffing ratios or professional (and educational) qualifications of staff, although these factors are important for other reasons.

However, the strongest relationship we uncovered with the quality of care provided by a home was the extent to which the head of home could specify a clear theoretical or therapeutic orientation, or at least methods of work for the home. This may be linked to the absence of Statements of Purpose. Not only were many homes unclear as to what they should be doing, they were also unsure how they were supposed to be doing it. Staff were therefore denied coherent explanations for why abused, neglected and rejected children behaved the way they did, and what a planned, establishment-wide response would constitute. Some staff told us how working with apparent chaos in children every day proved to be very frightening and sometimes personally detrimental. Homes had sometimes developed *administrative* systems, but planned, coherent *professional* procedures were more rare. In the least effective homes there was a tendency to adopt an *ad hoc* approach. There were thus contradictions and tensions between how different shifts and individual staff acted. While at one level manipulative children may revel in this, the experience of discontinuity, uncertainty and sometimes conflict in adults is unlikely to help them.

Freudian-based theory underpinned much of the development of modern social work and residential thinking (Balbernie 1996; Dockar-Drysdale 1968, 1973; Winnicott 1965), although such ideas are now less influential. Like us, the 'Warner' inquiry, in its national survey of children's homes, discovered therapeutic methods or techniques seldom being used with children (Department of Health 1992). Those it managed to detect were: behaviour modification and reward systems; normalisation programmes; group work; art/music therapy; social skills work; preparation for independence; and life story book work (p.226). It is not that any one of these methods is inherently more effective than another, but that some theoretical underpinning adds structure and coherence, consistency and explanations for staff. If something goes wrong, staff can then blame the theory rather than themselves. Even if homes told us that they were preparing adolescents for 'independence' (admittedly an unhelpful term) it was unusual for any sort of structured programme to exist, let alone, for example, an externally produced pack of resources or practice tools. Therefore, the overall programme often was not thought through; it was unclear at the outset exactly which areas were to be covered, when and by whom; and it was usually unspecified what the young person had to achieve before moving to the next stage. Preparation often focused on the cooker, ironing board and supermarket and disregarded much else. Others have considered this subject before, yet this wider thinking has been generally ignored.

Various explanations may be proposed as to why children's homes have not developed more focused working methods, although this is hardly an original observation. Indeed, the notion that they are intended to be therapeutic is probably a relatively recent development historically and, as far as adolescents are concerned, many politicians and members of the wider public would want to see them more as punitive agents of social control. One only has to recall the regular outcries in the media when it emerges that delinquents in residential care have been taken on summer holidays. The absence of coherent methods may also be linked to the general neglect of children's homes by local authority managers. Not all managers are necessarily expert in residential care. The rapid throughput of heads of homes also no doubt plays a part – we saw that most of our sample had joined their current establishment within the last year. It presumably takes some time to develop a distinctive approach and induct staff into its implementation, which is inhibited by constant reorganisations and transfer of senior staff. Lack of involvement in qualifying training may also make it more difficult to formulate a therapeutic approach and develop distinctive styles of work. Furthermore, there was sometimes a view that children's homes ('provider units') should provide what 'commissioners' stipulate. Commissioners may want different things, or not be clear about what it is that they require. Those with a fieldwork background may be unsympathetic to residential care in the first place or themselves favour a particular approach. All of this can make it difficult for a home to develop specific methods of work.

The multi-agency dimension

We end this report by focusing on three themes highlighted by the research that strike us as particularly significant. The first of these concerns the multi-agency dimension. As revealed in Chapter 4, young people looked after in residential accommodation clearly have multiple needs and problems. Social services departments are unable to tackle these in isolation. Thus young people may come into contact with, and need the help of, professionals in a wide variety of agencies including health, education, employment, housing, youth services, aftercare services, police and probation. With the exception of the group of disabled children, who are discussed below, it was evident in our study that relationships between social services and these other agencies were often problematic. Residential staff felt that multi-agency work generally had deteriorated in recent years.

Multi-agency work can take various forms. For example, it was noticeable that there was a general absence of specialist input in helping heads of homes and staff to plan the overall running of homes, including development of working methods and regimes. Consultants can be a mixed blessing but it seemed to us that the problems of children were often so acute, and their group management so challenging, that expert help was essential in devising appropriate strategies. Staff individually or collectively usually had no regular specialist support. Educational problems in the children's homes, therefore, were mostly addressed without specialist educational help. Clinical or educational psychologists were not involved in devising programmes of behavioural management. Staff often admitted that they felt completely out of their depth in trying to resolve major problems that had defeated others who were better equipped to cope.

We have also commented that children *individually* seemed to receive limited specialist help. Exceptions were with some younger children who were receiving counselling to deal with the effects of physical, sexual and emotional abuse, as well as to prepare for future moves. The situation, once again, was also different for children with severe learning disabilities (see below). Two private homes (L and J) made imaginative use of play and art therapy. Young people with offending histories were receiving little current input to address their criminality. The recent Audit Commission report (1996) on young people and crime has shown that the policy of cautioning is effective for juveniles before the pattern of offending becomes entrenched. However 'caution plus', where young people also receive some form of other intervention or service, is rare (p.23). The Audit Commission report is a major critique of the criminal justice system for young offenders, which it argues is highly inefficient and expensive. Overall it concludes that despite a rise in youth crime, less is done now than a decade ago to address offending by young people. It certainly appeared that little was being done to encourage and assist the young offenders we encountered to alter their behaviour.

Similarly, there was virtually no input from child psychologists or psychiatrists to help residents with their problems (the private home L was an exception). The need for more joint work between health and social services for children in need was highlighted in another Audit Commission report (1994). One study has pinpointed differences in time-scales between health and social work professionals, particularly regarding assessments, as an obstacle (Sinclair *et al.* 1995).

Educational liaison was similarly problematic. Links with schools varied depending on the quality of individual relationships: some heads and teachers were considered very helpful, others less so. Constructive joint policies between education and social services were frequently absent. Pupils who were excluded from school, or without places, received minimal input from education, usually no more than three to five hours a week. It is difficult to recall examples of educational psychologists working individually with children outside the assessment process and they would argue that resources prohibit this. Furthermore, education welfare officers/education social workers had little, if any, contact with our sample. It was rare for staff in these three social services departments to understand what role this service had in relation to children being looked after in residential care. It appeared that education welfare was likely to withdraw as social workers became more involved, but no one we encountered knew if this was actually the case and if so why.

Overall, therefore, we saw little evidence of a multi-professional response to meeting children's needs and no one agency had overall responsibility for co-ordination (Roaf and Lloyd 1995; Williams 1995). 'A policy for teenagers' approach was also absent (Department of Health 1996c; Triseliotis *et al.* 1995). Hopefully matters should improve as children's services plans become more firmly established, which emphasise co-operation and joint planning across departments. It will also be interesting to monitor the effects of new local government structures, as for example education and social services departments sometimes combine. Without some radical re-thinking and collective professional responsibility, which the Children Act 1989 stipulates, children's homes and social services in themselves are likely to have a very restricted impact on young people and their families' problems.

An alternative model of residential child care

A second major theme arising from our study stems from the two residential facilities we observed for children with severe learning disabilities. Interestingly, many of the above points did not apply and, instead, a quite different model of residential care existed. While in many ways the broad approach in these two units seemed superior to that offered elsewhere, this is not to suggest that services for disabled children and their families are in any way ideal. Families often experience financial problems. There is a great deal of unmet need, particularly involving minority ethnic groups, lone parent families and those catering for the most severely impaired children. Social work contact is often infrequent and many families feel unsupported (Beresford 1995). It has been estimated that only 5 per cent of disabled children use any form of short-term care, rising to 17 per cent of the most severely disabled group (reported in Robinson 1996a). Parents and children have generally expressed satisfaction with the short breaks they experience. However, there have been concerns over the quality of physical and personal care provided to some children, the behaviour of others, departure from normal routine and doubts about safety. There is also the problem of short-term care being unavailable when it is actually required (Robinson 1996a).

We should be cautious in inferring whether the differences we observed in the two homes offering short breaks were because of the underlying model of residential care, or was it simply that they were good individual homes? We do not believe it was merely the latter: one of the homes (I) scored well in our ratings but the other (H) did not (see Chapter 7). Yet between the homes there were still distinctive principles, assumptions and methods underlying the approach to child care.

Table 8.1 summarises the particular features underlying the approach to residential care observed in the two homes offering short breaks to disabled children. We have termed this an *enhanced, integrated model* of residential child care. One home was more effective at implementing this than the other. The table highlights mainly positive features of the model; shortcomings are discussed later.

Thus residential care for disabled children was provided strategically as a form of family support and shared care. A certain number of days of short-term care, specified in advance, was available for children and families to use. Home I was more flexible than home H in their allocation and the 'booking system' adopted. Residential care was part of a long-term plan to assist the family. None of our other ten homes offered care in this way. Instead, children in these other three categories of provision were admitted to residential care only in the midst of crisis or when family breakdown had already occurred. It has been stated that 'respite accommodation' is now more widely available for children without disabilities, encouraged by the Children Act 1989 (Aldgate *et al.* 1996). However, we did not encounter this in our other ten homes and an 'all or nothing' approach still tended to apply (Department of Health and Social Security 1985). Of course, services other than residential care may have been providing this. Nevertheless this was an important difference among our homes and the majority were inflexible in what they offered families.

Table 8.1 An enhanced, integrated model of residential child care: short-term breaks for young people with severe learning disabilities and additional health needs

Relationship with family

- short breaks as a form of family support and shared care
- a service for parents and children
- a break for *children* also seen as part of the package
- parents have power over, and involvement in, children's daily care
- liaison with parents to ensure consistency (for example, feeding, bedtimes and so on)
- different role of voluntary sector: more *individual* support for families.

Public/social attitudes

- cross-class; stigma issues are different
- higher status area of work; public recognition.

Inter-professional working

- good multi-agency planning and involvement; positive links with social workers
- greater consistency in professional approach
- all children go to school – exclusion not seen as an option. All pupils have statements of special educational need. Favourable teacher: pupil ratios
- special schools have positive approach to social services.

Nature of residential practice

- clear sense of purpose for units, to which they generally adhere
- work to structured programme, which is *expert-led*
- high level of individual interaction. Leisure activities used positively
- much 'normalising' activity
- children acquire instrumental skills
- staff demonstrate specialist skills, for example health care, physiotherapy
- staff demonstrate positive attitudes towards children. Reports are written positively and seek signs of progress
- focus on developmental issues rather than behaviour *per se* – a wider perspective.

Consequently, short breaks in these two homes were seen as a *service* to parents and children in need. Child protection issues were admittedly generally absent with the disabled children, which meant that the role of the local authority was different and oversight of the family was not required. However, support and the scrutiny of families are not mutually exclusive. Responsibility for children in the short breaks homes clearly remained with parents, who had a say in their daily care and stipulated certain arrangements, such as dress, diet and bedtime routine. In other homes, though relationships with parents were generally more positive than in the previous study, they did not have this degree of influence.

The question is often posed in relation to disabled children, exactly *for whom* is the short break provided? At least the earlier term 'respite care' was more honest and signalled that it was parents who essentially benefited, while separating child from home – albeit temporarily – may be unwelcome for the young person concerned. Residential services for young people without disabilities seem more child-centred in this respect. Yet paradoxically, these ten homes were often unsure what they should be doing with their residents once they arrived: we have already outlined the confusion over social work methods. In contrast, staff in the two homes offering short breaks were conscious that the interlude should also benefit the child and full use be made of the time away. It was therefore accepted that there should be high levels of interaction with children and emphasis on leisure activities. Attempts were made to provide children with experiences they would not routinely encounter, including 'normalising' activities in which they were interacting with children and adults without disabilities – going to the cinema, to parks, holiday camps and so on. Public attitudes, as we have seen, were often unwelcoming but staff saw it also as part of their responsibility to confront social barriers.

A major difference between disabled children and others in the study was the social profile of their families: children can be born with impairments in all sections of society, and disability, therefore, is cross-class. Other residents emanated from the poorest families (Bebbington and Miles 1989). Certainly we came across parents with disabled children who were affluent and articulate and complained if they were dissatisfied with the service they received; this was very unusual in other settings. The stigma issues, therefore, are quite different. There is also higher status allocated to those working with disabled children in residential settings compared with the wider group of children in need, which builds professional confidence.

It is relevant to note that in this model of care there is a strong inter-professional dimension. Health, education and social work professionals play a full part in devising care plans and care programmes. Children continue to see and receive help from specialists. Services, therefore, are *expert-led,* unlike the wider group we encountered. There are also marked educational contrasts: all pupils have statements of special educational need; all pupils attend school and exclusion is not considered an option; and there are favourable staffing levels in special schools.

This model of care also differed in aspects of residential practice. In addition to the points already made, there was emphasis on children acquiring instrumental skills, learning previously unfamiliar tasks. Staff could also themselves demonstrate specialist skills, such as in monitoring medical conditions and helping to provide physiotherapy – as part of care plans. Staff generally demonstrated positive attitudes towards children. Reports were written positively and sought signs of progress. Very importantly, there was a tendency not to lose sight of broader developmental objectives for children, nor to focus on behaviour *per se*. Thus although a considerable problem, staff did not become preoccupied with the subject of behaviour management at the expense of other goals (see Chapter 5).

The above are positive features of this model of care; there were also deficiencies. For example, we referred earlier to the ambivalence about parental contact when children were living in the residential home. Some discouragement of communication might therefore occur, which apart from specific circumstances did not generally happen in the other establishments. There is also the issue of consultation with disabled children and seeking their views about the experience. This would happen with residents more generally and, because children have impairments, this does not absolve us of the responsibility to involve them. Another problem of the short breaks homes was their large number of staff. Though providing greater scope for individual care, this also could lead to discontinuity and confusion. Furthermore, there are problems of public attitudes and the fact that impairments are often visible. Reactions and remarks to disabled children could be cruel and socially exclusive.

We should obviously be cautious in proposing an *enhanced, integrated model* of residential care on the basis of observations in such a small number of homes. Nonetheless, even allowing for differences in the extent to which it was implemented, there were clear contrasts and advantages in the fundamental approach to caring in the short breaks homes compared with the remainder. Loughran, Parker and Gordon (1992, Chapter 8) maintained that it is the unwillingness to accept emotional and behavioural problems and their effects as forms of disability that has prevented strong policy responses to these problems in the residential sector. We have termed this an 'integrated' model since it appears to be more complete: parents are involved, professionals play a full part, liaison is emphasised and the residential home knows what it is supposed to be doing. It is 'enhanced' because it seems progressive: it offers family support rather than simply dealing with its aftermath and enables residential staff to extend and utilise their skills.

Children's homes: development, decline or demise?

This leads to our final theme. The question the previous section rather begs is that, if we can apply an enhanced, integrated model of residential care in one category of home, why can this not be done – or at least significant parts of it – elsewhere, such as in work with adolescents? Indeed, the integrated model encompassing family support and involvement, multi-professional back-up and clarity of purpose, would be highly consistent with the positive role for residential care advocated by official reports (Wagner 1988; Department of Health 1991a), as well as guidance accompanying the Children Act 1989 (Department of Health 1991b). We also saw earlier that high quality care is provided in some settings – this is not restricted to certain categories, nor is it predetermined by the client group. As a society, therefore, we can provide good residential care if we wish.

We argued in the opening chapter that the disinclination to provide better services is long-standing. The history of residential care is tainted by the Poor Law, with notions of less eligibility and punitive deterrence, together with 'deserving' and 'undeserving' poor or 'allowed' and 'disallowed' dependencies. Our society is ambivalent about whether or not it genuinely wishes to help the occupants of children's homes and their families, particularly adolescents. The *meaning* of residential care varies depending on the client group. The class distinction evident in the current study, between services for children with disabilities and those without, brings this into sharp relief. It has been said that services for the poor tend to be poor services. Moral judgements are made about the poor, who are increasingly felt to be responsible for their situation. This is encouraged by neo-Conservative approaches to social welfare in which human happiness and freedom are to be obtained through the quest for independence (Dean 1995, Chapter 1). The more that society values individual success, the more personal failure is also highlighted. Perceptions of thresholds for age responsibility have also been reduced, fuelled by 'back to basics' moral crusades. In a time of profound social change, young people are increasingly targeted for public criticism, for example educational standards and disorderly behaviour (Berridge and Brodie 1997). While on the one hand we decry the neglect and abuse of children, sympathy does not extend so far as to make allowances for the 'looked after' population as they grow up.

Children's homes, therefore, are at the mercy of a range of external influences. The closure of larger, more specialist institutions – the disappearance of a whole tier of provision, in effect – has meant that they have inherited a more challenging clientele. They are attempting to deal with them in local open facilities, which no doubt potentially makes for better overall care but introduces additional control problems. Local authority managers continue to neglect residential homes. There is no evidence here that privately run homes as a group are any superior to local authority units, yet if public authorities are not prepared to support these adequately, as we have seen, they should hand over their management to someone who will. Wider social policy will continue to influence children's homes: for example, changes in education policy have disadvantaged children's homes' residents. The availability of jobs, training, benefits and housing affects the likelihood of family breakdown as well as future opportunities for current residents.

Some of the omens for children's homes are not good. Closures continue and this is part of a wider international trend, even in countries which, unlike England, value residential care for children and accord the work higher status. Reports emerge weekly of past physical and sexual abuse in children's homes, abetted by their 'social disconnectedness'. It is tempting for politicians and managers to rid themselves of the inconvenience and embarrassment. Numerous reports have now concluded that residential care has a positive contribution to make and should be seen as one of a range of options. Previous research, discussed in our opening chapter, also reveals that, comparing like with like, the contribution of residential care is not inferior to its main alternatives. If current developments persist, we are not confident that this message will continue to hold true (Sinclair and Gibbs 1996).

But even before these latest findings, attempts to portray a more positive image for children's homes have not been particularly successful. A week's planned PR campaign, predictably perhaps, was overshadowed by further disclosures of institutional abuse. Most social workers distrust residential care, instincts that are instilled and reinforced by their qualifying training. Agencies typically prohibit the use of residence unless all else has failed. Although, unlike in the USA, a placement policy of the 'least restrictive option' has not been reflected in English law (that is, family placements considered automatically in preference to residential care), this position has been arrived at implicitly. Furthermore, public attitudes to children's homes have hardened, encouraged by political rhetoric and recent Conservative governments' mistrust of social work, social work values and social workers.

It has been shown that the unpopularity and decline of residential child care goes back a very long way, certainly to the early nineteenth century (Gooch 1996). Its development and use has depended on the availability of alternatives. As the volume of residential care declines, it is not immediately obvious what alternatives are being put in its place. Family support services have been insufficiently developed as, for professional and political reasons, social work in the past has overemphasised child protection rather than general services for children in need (Department of Health 1995; Parton 1996). Unlike other areas, such as perhaps child protection or services for under eights, work with adolescents lacks coherence and inter-agency policies for teenagers are generally lacking (Department of Health 1996c). Concerns have been raised by the

Association of Directors of Social Services (1997) about the current situation of foster care, including the retention and recruitment of carers. The provision of family placements for adolescents is very patchy (Berridge 1997; Triseliotis *et al.* 1995). Indeed, the situation is said to have reached crisis point in parts of the USA, where during a period in which the number of children entering public care rose by a third, the supply of foster carers *fell* by the same proportion (Mayers Pasztor and Wynne 1995; Morton 1995). There are no grounds for complacency towards foster care in this country. Waiting lists exist for family-link services for disabled children, with most carers being described as white and middle class (Beckford and Robinson 1993).

Thus it does not seem that viable alternatives to residential care are plentiful. Of course this assumes that children in need should receive a service, whereas social policy in the 1980s and 90s has moved in the direction of individuals and families assuming greater responsibility for their own welfare and universal social services being restricted or denied – for example, public housing, care of the elderly, school exclusions, student grants, asylum seekers and, one might add, young offenders.

Revisiting children's homes after a decade, therefore, has aroused mixed feelings. Some things have improved, others worsened. Residential homes for children constitute a unique social world and certain children, staff and situations will not be easily forgotten. We have shown that children's homes are more varied than many commentators have assumed. Positive models of care were found in the homes offering short breaks and those for younger children. There was more confusion about objectives and working methods concerning adolescents. We now know a great deal from research studies and previous practice about how residential care should optimally be organised. However, this is no guarantee that it will permanently benefit residents in the longer term: it is one influence among many and usually of brief duration. Despite this, we feel that society has a continuing obligation to provide high quality, enriching experiences for the young who have been seriously disadvantaged. Up-to-date knowledge has an important part to play in this.

References

Abel-Smith, B. and Titmuss, K. (1987) *The Philosophy of Welfare: Selected Writings of Richard M. Titmuss.* London: Allen and Unwin.

Alderson, P. (1995) *Listening to Children: Children, Ethics and Social Research.* Barkingside: Barnardo's.

Aldgate, J., Bradley, M. and Hawley, D. (1996) 'Respite accommodation: a case study of partnership under the Children Act 1989.' In M. Hill and J. Aldgate (eds) *Child Welfare Services: Developments in Law, Policy and Practice.* London: Jessica Kingsley.

Aldgate, J., Maluccio, A. and Reeves, C. (1989) *Adolescents in Foster Families.* London: Batsford.

Ames Reed, J. (1993) *We Have Learned a Lot from Them.* Barkingside: Barnardo's/National Children's Bureau.

Association of Directors of Social Services (1997) *The Foster Care Market: A National Perspective.* Ipswich: Suffolk Social Services.

Audit Commission (1994) *Seen But Not Heard: Co-Ordinating Community Child Health and Social Services for Children in Need.* London: HMSO.

Audit Commission (1996) *Misspent Youth: Young People and Crime.* London: Audit Commission.

Balbernie, R. (1966) *Residential Work with Children.* Brighton: Human Context Books.

Barclay Committee (1982) *Social Workers: Their Role and Tasks.* London: Bedford Square Press.

Barker, R. (1996) 'Child protection, public services and the chimera of market force efficiency.' *Children & Society 10,* 28–39.

Barnado's (1995) *The Facts of Life: The Changing Face of Childhood.* Barkingside: Barnado's.

Barter, C. (forthcoming) *Investigating Institutional Abuse of Children: An Exploration of the NSPCC Experience* (Provisional title). London: NSPCC.

Barter, C. (1997) Who's to blame? Conceptualising institutional abuse by children. *Early Child Development and Care, 133,* 101–114.

Bebbington, A. and Miles, J. (1989) 'The background of children who enter local authority care.' *British Journal of Social Work 19,* 5, 349–368.

Becker, H. (1963) *Outsiders.* Glencoe: Free Press.

Beckford, V. and Robinson, C. (1993) *Consolidation or Change? A Second Survey of Family Based Respite Care Services in the UK.* Bristol: Shared Care UK.

Beresford, B. (1995) *Expert Opinions: A National Survey of Parents Caring for a Severely Disabled Child.* Bristol: Policy Press.

Berridge, D. (1985) *Children's Homes.* Oxford: Basil Blackwell.

Berridge, D. (1994) 'Foster and residential care reassessed: a research perspective.' *Children & Society 8,* 2, 132–150.

Berridge, D. (1995a) *Power and Values in Child Welfare Research: An Underview.* Professorial Inaugural Lecture. Luton: University of Luton.

Berridge, D. (1995b) 'Families in need: crisis and responsibility.' In H. Dean (ed) *Parents' Duties, Children's Debts: The Limits of Policy Intervention.* Aldershot: Ashgate Publishing.

Berridge, D. (1997) *Foster Care: A Research Review.* London: The Stationery Office.

Berridge, D. and Brodie, I. (1996) 'Residential child care in England and Wales: the enquiries and after.' In M. Hill and J. Aldgate (eds) *Child Welfare Services: Developments in Law, Policy and Practice.* London: Jessica Kingsley.

Berridge, D. and Brodie, I. (1997) 'An exclusive education.' *Community Care 1156,* 30 January, 4–5.

Berridge, D. and Cleaver, H. (1987) *Foster Home Breakdown.* Oxford: Basil Blackwell.

Berridge, D. and Wenman, H. (1995) 'Involving children's centre residents in recruiting a university researcher.' *Children UK 4,* 12–14.

Berridge, D., Barrett, D., Brodie, I., Henderson, B. and Wenman, H. (1995) *Cautious Optimism? Changing Residential Care in a Local Authority.* Warwick: University of Warwick/Social Care Association.

Berridge, D., Brodie, I., Ayre, P., Barrett, D., Henderson, B. and Wenman, H. (1997) *Hello – Is Anybody Listening? The Education of Young People in Residential Care.* Warwick: University of Warwick/Social Care Association.

Biehal, N., Clayden, J., Stein, M. and Wade, J. (1992) *Prepared for Living? A Survey of Young People Leaving the Care of Three Local Authorities.* London: National Children's Bureau.

Blatt, E. (1992) 'Factors associated with child abuse and neglect in residential care settings.' *Children and Youth Services Review 14,* 493–517.

Bourne, J., Bridges, L. and Searle, C. (1994) *Outcast England: How Schools Exclude Black Children.* London: Institute of Race Relations.

Bradshaw, J. (1990) *Child Poverty and Deprivation in the UK.* London: National Children's Bureau.

Bradshaw, J. (1996) 'Poverty and deprivation in the United Kingdom.' *Research, Policy and Planning 14,* 1, 4–14.

Brannen, J. (ed) (1992) *Mixing Methods: Qualitative and Quantitative Research.* Aldershot: Avebury.

Brodie, I. (1995) 'Exclusion from school.' *Highlight* series. London: National Children's Bureau.

Brodie, I. and Berridge, D. (1996) *Exclusion From School: Research Themes and Issues.* Luton: University of Luton Press.

Brodie, I., Berridge, D. and Beckett, W. (1997) 'The health of children looked after by local authorities.' *British Journal of Nursing 6,* 7, 386–390.

Brown, E., Bullock, R., Hobson, C. and Little, M. (forthcoming) *Structure and Culture of Children's Homes.* Aldershot: Ashgate.

Bryman, A. and Cramer, D. (1990) *Quantitative Data Analysis for Social Scientists.* London: Routledge and Kegan Paul.

Bullock, R., Little, M. and Millham, S. (1993a) *Residential Care for Children: A Review of the Research.* London: HMSO.

Bullock, R., Little, M. and Millham, S. (1993b) *Going Home: The Return of Children Separated from their Families.* Aldershot: Dartmouth.

Butler-Sloss, Lord Justice E. (1988) *Report of the Inquiry into Child Abuse in Cleveland 1987.* Cm 412. London: Department of Health and Social Security.

Caprara, G. and Rutter, M. (1995) 'Individual development and social change.' In M. Rutter and D. Smith (eds) *Psychosocial Disorders in Young People: Time Trends and their Causes.* Chichester: Wiley.

Carlen, P., Gleeson, D. and Wardhaugh, J. (1992) *Truancy: The Politics of Compulsory Schooling.* Buckingham: Open University Press.

Cawson, P. (1978) *Community Homes: A Study of Residential Staff.* London: HMSO.

Chartered Institute of Public Finance and Accountancy (1996) *Personal Social Services Statistics 1994–95, Actuals.* London: CIPFA.

Cheetham, J., Fuller, R., McIvor, G. and Petch, A. (1992) *Evaluating Social Work Effectiveness.* Buckingham: Open University Press.

Cheung, S. and Heath, A. (1994) 'After care: the education and occupation of adults who have been in care.' *Oxford Review of Education 20,* 3, 361–374.

Clarke, G. and Cooke, D. (1983) *A Basic Course in Statistics.* London: Edward Arnold.

Cliffe, D. with Berridge, D. (1991) *Closing Children's Homes: An End To Residential Childcare?* London: National Children's Bureau.

Colton, M. (1988) *Dimensions of Substitute Care: A Comparative Study of Foster and Residential Care Practice.* Aldershot: Avebury.

Community Care (1996) 1151, 19 December, 3.

Cramer, D. (1994) *Introducing Statistics for Social Research.* London: Routledge.

Dean, H. (ed) (1995) *Parents' Duties, Children's Debts: The Limits of Policy Intervention.* Aldershot: Ashgate Publishing.

Department for Education and Employment (1993) 'A new deal for "out of school" pupils.' Press Release 126/33.

Department of Education and Science (1980) *Community Homes with Education.* London: HMSO.

Department of Health (1989) *An Introduction to the Children Act 1989.* London: HMSO.

Department of Health (1991a) *Children in the Public Care: A Review of Residential Care.* London: HMSO.

Department of Health (1991b) *The Children Act 1989. Guidance and Regulations: Volume 4 – Residential Care.* London: HMSO.

Department of Health (1991c) *The Children Act 1989. Guidance and Regulations: Volume 6 – Children with Disabilities.* London: HMSO.

Department of Health (1991d) *Patterns and Outcomes in Child Placement: Messages from Current Research and their Implications.* London: HMSO.

Department of Health (1992) *Choosing with Care: The Report of the Committee of Inquiry into the Selection, Development and Management of Staff in Children's Homes.* London: HMSO.

Department of Health (1993) *Guidance on Permissible Forms of Control in Children's Residential Care.* London: Department of Health.

Department of Health (1995a) *Child Protection: Messages From Research.* London: HMSO.

Department of Health (1995b) *Looking After Children.* London: HMSO.

Department of Health (1996a) *Children Looked After by Local Authorities. Year Ending 31 March 1995, England.* London: Department of Health.

Department of Health (1996b) *Children's Homes at 31 March 1996, England.* London: Department of Health.

Department of Health (1996c) *Focus on Teenagers.* London: HMSO.

Department of Health (1996d) *Taking Care, Taking Control.* Training video. London: Department of Health.

Department of Health (1997) *The Control of Children in the Public Care.* London: Department of Health.

Department of Health and Social Security (1985) *Social Work Decisions in Child Care: Recent Research Findings and their Implications.* London: HMSO.

Department of Health Social Services Inspectorate (1994a) *Inspection of Residential Child Care Services in 11 Local Authorities.* London: Department of Health.

Department of Health Social Services Inspectorate (1994b) *Services to Disabled Children and their Families: Report of the National Inspection of Services to Disabled Children and their Families.* London: Department of Health.

Department of Health Social Services Inspectorate (1995a) *Independent Fostering Agencies Study.* London: Department of Health.

Department of Health Social Services Inspectorate (1995b) *Small Unregistered Children's Homes.* London: Department of Health.

Department of Health Social Services Inspectorate (1996) *Inspection of Local Authority Fostering 1995–96.* London: Department of Health.

Department of Health Social Services Inspectorate and Office for Standards in Education (1995) *The Education of Children Who Are Looked After by Local Authorities.* London: Department of Health Social Services Inspectorate and Office for Standards in Education.

Department of Health and Social Services Northern Ireland (1986) *Committee of Inquiry into Children's Homes and Hostels.* Belfast: DHSS.

Devlin, A. (1996) *Criminal Classes.* Winchester: Waterside Press.

Dey, I. (1993) *Qualitative Data Analysis.* London: Routledge and Kegan Paul.

Dockar-Drysdale, B. (1968) *Therapy in Child Care.* London: Longman.

Dockar-Drysdale, B. (1973) *Consultation in Child Care.* London: Longman.

Douglas, M. (1975) *Implicit Meanings: Essays in Anthropology.* London: Routledge and Kegan Paul.

Eichler, M. (1988) *Non-Sexist Research Methods: A Practical Guide.* London: Routledge and Kegan Paul.

Ferri, E. and Smith, P. (1996) *Parenting in the 1990s.* London: Family Policy Studies Centre.

Fine, G. and Sandstrom, K. (1988) *Knowing Children: Participant Observation with Minors.* Qualitative Research Methods Series 15. Newbury Park: Sage.

Fletcher-Campbell, F. and Hall, C. (1990) *Changing Schools? Changing People? A Study of the Education of Children in Care.* Windsor: National Foundation for Educational Research/Nelson.

Fogelman, K. (1976) *Britain's Sixteen-Year-Olds.* London: National Children's Bureau.

Fombonne, E. (1996) 'Depressive disorders: time trends and possible explanatory mechanisms.' In M. Rutter and D. Smith (eds.) *Psychosocial Disorders in Young People: Time Trends and Their Causes.* Chichester: Wiley.

Fox Harding, L. (1991) *Perspectives in Child Care Policy.* London: Longman.

Frost, N. and Stein, M. (1989) *The Politics of Child Welfare: Inequality, Power and Change.* London: Harvester Wheatsheaf.

Gans, H. (1982) 'The participant observer as a human being: observations on the personal aspects of fieldwork.' In R. Burgess (ed) *Field Research: A Sourcebook and Field Manual.* Contemporary Social Research No. 4. London: Routledge and Kegan Paul.

Garnett, L. (1992) *Leaving Care and After.* London: National Children's Bureau.

Gibbons, J. Conroy, S. and Bell, C. (1995) *Operating the Child Protection System.* London: HMSO.

Gillborn, D. and Gipps, C. (1996) *Recent Research on the Achievements of Ethnic Minority Pupils.* London: HMSO.

Glaser, B. (1978) *Theoretical Sensitivity.* Mill Valley: Sociology Press.

Glaser, B. and Strauss, A. (1967) *The Discovery of Grounded Theory.* Chicago: Aldine.

Goffman, E. (1968) *Asylums.* Harmondsworth: Penguin.

Gooch, D. (1996) 'Home and away: the residential care, education and control of children in historical and political context.' *Child and Family Social Work 1,* 19–32.

Gould, N. (1989) 'Reflective learning for social work practice.' *Social Work Education 8,* 2, 9–19.

Graham, J. and Bowling, B. (1995) *Young People and Crime.* Research Study 145. London: Home Office.

Grimshaw, R. with Berridge, D. (1994) *Educating Disruptive Children: Placement and Progress in Residential Special Schools for Pupils with Emotional and Behavioural Difficulties.* London: National Children's Bureau.

Hales, G. (ed) (1996) *Beyond Disability: Towards an Enabling Society.* London: Sage.

Halsey, A. (1992) 'Changes in the family.' *Children & Society 7,* 2, 125–136.

Harrison, S. and Wistow, G. (1992) 'The purchaser/provider split in English health care: towards explicit rationing?' *Policy and Politics 20,* 2, 123–130.

Haskey, J. (1996) 'The proportion of married couples who divorce.' *Population Trends 83,* 25–36.

Hayden, C., Sheppard, D. and Ward, C. (1996) *Primary Age Children Excluded From School.* Report No. 33. Portsmouth: University of Portsmouth.

Heath, A., Colton, M. and Aldgate, J. (1994) 'Failure to escape: a longitudinal study of foster children's educational attainment.' *British Journal of Social Work 24,* 3, 241–260.

Hill, M., Laybourn, A. and Borland, M. (1996) 'Engaging with primary-aged children about their emotions and well-being: methodological considerations.' *Children & Society 10,* 2, 129–144.

Home Office, Department of Health, Department of Education and Science and Welsh Office (1991) *Working Together Under the Children Act 1989.* London: HMSO.

Humphreys, L. (1970) *Tearoom Trade.* London: Duckworth.

Jackson, S. (1987) *The Education of Children in Care.* Bristol: University of Bristol, School of Applied Social Studies.

Jackson, S. (1989) 'Residential care and education.' *Children & Society 2,* 4, 335–350.

Jones, A. and Bilton, K. (1994) *The Future Shape of Children's Services.* London: National Children's Bureau.

Jones, J. (1994) 'Towards an understanding of power relationships in institutional abuse.' *Early Child Development and Care 100,* 69–76.

Jones, J. (1995) 'Institutional abuse: understanding domination from the inside looking out.' *Early Child Development and Care 113,* 85–92.

Kahan, B. (1994) *Growing Up in Groups*. London: HMSO.

Kendrick, A. (1995) *Residential Care in the Integration of Child Care Services*. Central Research Unit Papers. Edinburgh: The Scottish Office.

Kennedy, M. (1996) 'Children with disabilities and child protection.' *Highlight* series. London: National Children's Bureau.

Kinnear, P. and Gray, C. (1994) *SPSS for Windows Made Simple*. Hove: Lawrence Erlbaum.

Kirkwood, A. (1993) *The Leicestershire Inquiry 1992*. Leicester: Leicestershire County Council.

Knapp, M. and Robinson, E. (1989) 'The cost of services.' In B. Kahan (ed) *Child Care Research, Policy and Practice*. London: Hodder and Stoughton.

Kumar, V. (1993) *Poverty and Inequality in the UK: The Effects on Children*. London: National Children's Bureau.

Layder, D. (1993) *New Strategies in Social Research*. Cambridge: Polity Press.

Le Grand, J. and Bartlett, W. (1993) *Quasi-Markets and Social Policy*. Hampshire: Macmillan Press.

Lee, R. (1993) *Doing Research on Sensitive Topics*. London: Sage.

Levy, A. and Kahan, B. (1991) *The Pindown Experience and the Protection of Children*. Stafford: Staffordshire County Council.

Little, M. (1995) *A Life Without Problems? The Achievements of a Therapeutic Community*. Aldershot: Arena.

Little, M. and Gibbons, J. (1993) 'Predicting the rate of children on the child protection register.' *Research, Policy and Planning 10*, 2, 15–18.

Loughran, F., Parker, R. and Gordon, D. (1992) *Children with Disabilities in Communal Establishments: A Further Analysis and Interpretation of the Office of Population, Censuses and Surveys' Investigation*. Bristol: University of Bristol, Department of Social Policy and Planning.

Madge, N. (1994) *Children and Residential Care in Europe*. London: National Children's Bureau.

Marsh, P. and Triseliotis, J. (1996) *Ready to Practice? Social Workers and Probation Officers: Their Training and First Year in Work*. Aldershot: Avebury.

Marshall, C. and Rossman, G. (1995) *Designing Qualitative Research*. London: Sage.

Mayers Pasztor, E. and Wynne, S. (1995) *Foster Parent Retention and Recruitment: The State of the Art in Practice and Policy*. Washington, DC: Child Welfare League of America.

McCall, G. and Simmons, J. (1969) *Issues in Participant Observation: A Text and Reader*. Reading, Massachussetts: Addison-Wesley.

McCann, J. and Jones, A. (1996) Paper presented to the Association of Child Psychologists and Psychiatrists conference, Midlands branch, 10 October 1996

McCracken, G. (1988) *The Long Interview*. London: Sage.

Mennell, S., Murcott, A. and van Otterloo, A. (1992) *The Sociology of Food: Eating, Diet and Culture*. London: Sage.

Millham, S., Bullock, R. and Cherrett, P. (1979) *After Grace – Teeth: A Comparative Study of the Residential Experience of Boys in Approved Schools*. Brighton: Chaucer.

Millham, S., Bullock, R. and Hosie, K. (1980) *Learning to Care*. Farnborough: Gower.

Millham, S., Bullock, R., Hosie, K. and Haak, M. (1986) *Lost in Care*. Aldershot: Gower.

Mintel (1996) *Pre-Family Lifestyles*. London: Mintel.

Morrow, V. and Richards, M. (1996) *Transitions to Adulthood: A Family Matter?* York: York Publishing Services Ltd.

Morton, T. (1995) 'The evolution of foster care in a caring society.' Paper presented to International Foster Care Conference, 25 July 1995, Bergen, Norway.

National Consumer Council (NCC) and Who Cares? Trust (1993) *Not Just a Name: The Views of Young People in Foster and Residential Care.* London: National Consumer Council.

Office of Population, Censuses and Surveys (1989) *Disabled Children: Services, Transport and Education.* London: HMSO.

Office of Population, Censuses and Surveys (1996) *General Household Survey 1994.* London: OPCS.

Office for Standards in Education (1995) *Pupil Referral Units: The First Twelve Inspections.* London: HMSO.

Oliver, M. (1990) *The Politics of Disablement.* London: Macmillan.

Osborn, A. and St Clair, L. (1987) 'The ability and behaviour of children who have been in care or separated from their parents.' *Early Child Development and Care 28*, 3, 187–354.

Oswin, M. (1984) *They Keep Going Away.* Oxford: Basil Blackwell/King's Fund.

Packman, J. and Jordan, B. (1991) The Children Act: looking forward, looking back. *Children & Society 21*, 4, 315–327.

Packman, J., Randall, J. and Jacques, N. (1986) *Who Needs Care? Social Work Decisions About Children.* Oxford: Basil Blackwell.

Parker, R. (1990) *Away from Home: A History of Child Care.* Barkingside: Barnardo's.

Parker, R. and Loughran, F. (1990) *Trends in Child Care.* Bristol: University of Bristol, School of Applied Social Studies.

Parker, R., Ward, H., Jackson, S., Aldgate, J. and Wedge, P. (1991) *Looking After Children: Assessing Outcomes in Child Care.* London: HMSO.

Parsons, C. (1996) 'Permanent exclusions from schools in England in the 1990s: trends, causes and responses.' *Children and Society 10*, 177–186.

Parsons, R. (1995) *The Sixty Minute Father.* Cardiff: Headline.

Parton, N. (1991) *Governing the Family: Child Care, Child Protection and the State.* Basingstoke: Macmillan.

Parton, N. (1994) 'The nature of social work under conditions of (post) modernity.' *Social Work and Social Services Review 5*, 2, 93–112.

Parton, N. (1996) 'Child protection, family support and social work: a critical appraisal of the Department of Health research studies in child protection.' *Child and Family Social Work 1*, 3–11.

Pilling, D. (1990) *Escape from Disadvantage.* London: Falmer Press.

Pinchbeck, I. and Hewitt, M. (1973) *Children in English Society.* London: Routledge and Kegan Paul.

Pitts, J. (forthcoming) 'Youth crime, social change and social class in Britain and France in the 1980s and 1990s.' In H. Jones (ed) *Towards a Classless Society.* London: Routledge and Kegan Paul.

Polsky, N. (1967) *Hustlers, Beats and Others.* Chicago: Aldine.

Quinton, D. and Rutter, M. (1984) 'Parents with children in care. Intergenerational continuities.' *Journal of Child Psychology and Psychiatry 25*, 231–250.

Renzetti, C. and Lee, R. (1993) *Researching Sensitive Topics.* London: Sage.

Roaf, C. and Lloyd, C. (1995) *The Welfare Network: How Well Does the Net Work?* Occasional Paper 6. Oxford: Oxford Brookes University.

Robinson, C. (1996a) 'Breaks for disabled children.' In K. Stalker (ed) *Developments in Short-Term Care: Breaks and Opportunities.* London: Jessica Kingsley.

Robinson, C. (1996b) 'Short-term care for children.' *Child and Family Social Work 1*, 261–266.

Robinson, C., Weston, C. and Minkes, J. (1994) *Assessing Quality in Services to Disabled Children under the Children Act 1989.* Bristol: University of Bristol, Norah Fry Research Centre.

Robinson, C., Weston, C. and Minkes, J. (1996) *Quality in Residential Short-Term Care Services.* London: The Stationery Office.

Rowe, J. and Lambert, L. (1973) *Children Who Wait.* London: Association of British Adoption Agencies.

Rowe, J., Hundleby, M. and Garnett, L. (1989) *Child Care Now: A Survey of Placement Patterns.* London: British Agencies for Adoption and Fostering.

Russell, P. (1996) 'Short-term care. Parental perspectives.' In K. Stalker (ed) *Developments in Short-Term Care.* London: Jessica Kingsley.

Schön, D. (1983) *The Reflective Practitioner: How Professionals Think in Action.* London: Arena.

Schorr, A. (1992) *The Personal Social Services: An Outside View.* York: Joseph Rowntree Foundation.

Silverman, D. (1993) *Interpreting Qualitative Data.* London: Sage.

Sinclair, I. (1971) *Hostels for Probationers.* London: HMSO.

Sinclair, I. and Gibbs, I. (1996) *Quality of Care in Children's Homes.* Report to the Department of Health. York: University of York.

Sinclair, R., Garnett, L. and Berridge, D. (1995) *Social Work and Assessment with Adolescents.* London: National Children's Bureau.

Smith, E. (1995) 'Bring back the orphanages.' *Child Welfare 74*, 1, 115–142.

Social Services Inspectorate, Wales and Social Information Systems (1991) *Accommodating Children: A Review of Children's Homes in Wales.* Cardiff: Welsh Office.

Social Research Association (1994) *Social Research Ethical Guidelines.* Appendix B. London: Social Research Association.

Spencer, J. and Flyn, R. (1990) *The Evidence of Children: The Law and Psychology.* London: Blackstone.

Stalker, K. and Robinson, C. (1991) *You're on the Waiting List. Families Waiting for Respite Care Services.* Bristol: University of Bristol, Norah Fry Research Centre.

Stein, M. and Carey, K. (1986) *Leaving Care.* Oxford: Basil Blackwell.

Stirling, M. (1992) 'How many pupils are being excluded?' *British Journal of Special Education 19*, 4, 128–130.

Strathdee, R. and Johnson, M. (1994) *Out of Care and on the Streets: Young People, Care Leavers and Homelessness.* London: Centrepoint.

The Times 10 June 1996, 10.

The Times 28 January 1995, 6.

Townsley, R. and Macadam, M. (1996) *Choosing Staff: Involving People with Learning Difficulties in Staff Recruitment.* Bristol: Policy Press.

Triseliotis, J., Borland, M., Hill, M. and Lambert, L. (1995) *Teenagers and the Social Work Services.* London: HMSO.

Triseliotis, J., Sellick, C. and Short, R. (1995) *Foster Care: Theory and Practice.* London: Batsford.

Triseliotis, J., Shireman, J. and Hundleby, M. (1997) *Adoption: Theory, Policy and Practice.* London: Cassell.

Troyna, B. and Hatcher, R. (1992) *Racism in Children's Lives.* London: Routledge and Kegan Paul in association with the National Children's Bureau.

United Nations (1989) *The Convention on the Rights of the Child.* Geneva: UN.

Wagner, G. (1988) *Residential Care: A Positive Choice.* London: HMSO.

Ward, H. (ed) (1995) *Looking After Children: Research into Practice.* London: HMSO.

Waterhouse, S. (1997) *The Organisation of Fostering Services: A Study of the Arrangements for the Delivery of Fostering Services in England.* London: National Foster Care Association.

Westcott, H. and Cross, M. (1996) *This Far and No Further: Towards Ending the Abuse of Disabled Children.* London: Venture Press.

Whitaker, D., Archer, L. and Hicks, L. (1996) *The Prevailing Cultures and Staff Dynamics in Children's Homes.* York: University of York, Social Work Research and Development Unit.

Williams, E. (1995) 'Falling through the net.' *Search 24,* 5–7.

Winnicott, D. (1965) *The Family and Individual Development.* London: Tavistock.

Wistow, G., Knapp, M., Hardy, B. and Allen, C. (1992) 'From providing to enabling: local authorities and the mixed economy of social care.' *Public Administration 70,* 25–45.

Subject Index

Author Index